Brendan's Return Voyage

A New American Dream

Brendan's Return Voyage

A New American Dream

Indigenous, Post-Colonial, and Celtic Theology

Ray Simpson

RESOURCE *Publications* • Eugene, Oregon

BRENDAN'S RETURN VOYAGE: A NEW AMERICAN DREAM
Indigenous, Post-Colonial, and Celtic Theology

Resource Publications
An Imprint of Wipf and Stock Publishers
199 W. 8th Ave., Suite 3
Eugene, OR 97401

www.wipfandstock.com

PAPERBACK ISBN: 978-1-7252-9209-3
HARDCOVER ISBN: 978-1-7252-9210-9
EBOOK ISBN: 978-1-7252-9211-6

03/12/21

Contents

1

———

The Brendan Voyage to America

A Parable for Our Time

AMERICA IS POLARIZED. YET globalists and localists, indigenous tribes and settlers alike fear coming conflict and ecological disasters. The world-view that dominated the twentieth century crumbles. What will take its place? Can a new generation of indigenous and more recent Americans cut away centuries of false baggage and travel the Way together?

I am not an expert on White America nor on its Indigenous Peoples: I am a pilgrim who has come to seek the Creator's imprints in all its peoples—indigenous and settlers.

My US friend Will Toms lost his father at the age of five and had an abusive stepfather. As an adult he had a vision of an Indian chief whom he invited to be his father. Will and his wife Millie, who follow Jesus, got a call to ministry among pre-European native peoples. They established the YWAM Tribal Winds ministry. Although white Christians have started many churches among native tribes, too often they have failed to look for the Creator's imprints in those tribes and have told Indian converts to ditch their culture and adopt the white person's ways. Will and Millie thought that was wrong.

Someone told Will a story that in ancient times a holy man named Brendan sailed from Ireland in a boat made of wood and skins and landed in North America. He followed the One whose name white people translate as Jesus. He may have intended to colonize, to establish a new paradise like the Garden of Eden in this foreign land. However, when Brendan met the native people he realized that his Jesus was already among them, so, with humility he sailed all the way back to Ireland!

Will thought to himself, "We need a new Brendan, because now we are blind to the Creator's imprints in Indian tribes and we are defacing the Creator's imprints in White society". Then he learned of a movement that includes white Americans who are inspired by Brendan to follow humble ways. They make this vow: "I undertake to follow a rhythm of prayer, work and re-creation . . . to live simply that others may simply live . . ." They make the vow in a ceremony called The Voyage of the Coracle. Words from Brendan's Voyage are read and a guardian says "God is calling you to leave behind everything that stops you setting sail in the ocean of God's love . . . Be ready for the Spirit to lead you into wild, windy or well-worn places in the knowledge that God will make them places of wonder and welcome. God is giving us the vision of a spoiled creation being restored to harmony with its Creator, of a fragmented world becoming whole, of a weakened church being restored to its mission, of lands being healed and lit up by the glorious Trinity."

Some of these new Brendans band together in the dispersed international Community of Aidan and Hilda. Its first US Guardian, Revd. Jack Stapleton, was drawn to the Community's commitment to "healing of the land". Stapleton wrote:

> Indians have been historically resistant to what they see as the white man's religion. And thank God they have been. It is a tragedy that so many Native Americans have not known the saving and redeeming power of Jesus Christ. But by resisting both the Western form of Christianity and the values of Western culture, they have created a space in their own cultural life where a new, radical form of the Gospel, a form not unlike Celtic Christianity, may be birthed.

Will wondered "Could such new movements help white, black, and native Americans to shed proud, unexamined ways, and journey together to a better future, allowing the One who is among them to teach them afresh?"

This is not a wholly new idea. In 1987 the philosopher Alasdair MacIntyre painted a bleak picture of trends in the American way of life, which he thought might lead to a new Dark Age. He called for "a new Benedict"—though he thought this new type of monastic would be unlike the first Benedict. This has led to fresh thinking, publicized in books such as *The Benedict Option* in 2017. In this book conservative columnist Rod

Dreher calls on American Christians to prepare for the coming Dark Age by embracing an ancient Christian way of life.

I think the *Brendan Option* offers a better paradigm, because Brendan embraces movement more than stability, intuition as much as reason, and, unlike Benedict, he worked outside the framework of empire, planting the Gospel within the natural patterns of the indigenous people.

In 1963 President John F. Kennedy said: "Before we can set out on the road to success we have to know where we are going; and before we can know that, we must determine where we have been in the past. It seems a basic requirement to study the history of our Indian people. America has much to learn about the heritage of our American Indians. Only through this study can we as a nation do what must be done if our treatment of the American Indians is not to be marked down for all time as a national disgrace."[1]

What is a new idea is that Euro-Americans who get a conscience about diseased roots in the western soul can rediscover the wellsprings of their own forebears' indigenous Celtic tribes and be changed by them, thus also finding life-giving bonds with their Indian brothers and sisters as we enter the new era that lies ahead. A majority of Europeans who colonized North America came from the Celtic western fringes of their continent: Ireland, Britain, Spain and France. Gaul (which became France), Galicia (the part of Spain which hosts The Camino Way to Santiago), and Scots and Irish Gaelic have a similar root, as does the ancient Asian province of Galatia to whom the apostle Paul addressed his letter. The story of how the ways of Jesus took root among those indigenous Celtic tribes in a more relational way than the regulatory approach of the Roman Empire is like reading The Acts of the Apostles Volume Two.

So, this book will do four things:

- provide a few examples of the Creator's imprints in indigenous tribes;
- pinpoint some things in western culture and western missions that need to be repented of, but also some of the Creator's imprints in them;
- highlight features of Jesus in Celtic spirituality that can become a transforming element in our life streams today;
- suggest a way we can voyage together into the future in the spirit of Brendan

I am just a pilgrim who has:

---

1. Twiss, *One Church Many Tribes*

- accepted invitations to learn from a few First Nation peoples in Australia, Canada, and USA and to give teaching to some of them.

- searched to identify the root diseases that spoil the western world[2]

- engaged in thirty years' research into the spirituality of ancient Celtic indigenous tribes in the Western World.

May this book change us.

2. Simpson *The Cowshed Revolution*

2

The Creator's Imprints in Indigenous Tribes

"Elohim has made of one blood all the tribes on earth."

ACTS 17:26.

"What may be known about God has been made known to them. For since the creation of the world God's invisible qualities—his eternal power and divine nature—have been clearly seen."

ROMANS 1:19.

"After this I saw a great multitude that no one could number, from every nation, from all tribes and peoples and languages, standing before the throne and before the Lamb, clothed in white robes . . . All the tribes worshipped and brought of their treasures before the Lamb with palm branches in their hands".

REVELATION 7:9.

Grandfather, Wakan-Tanka! You have been always, and before you nothing has been. There is no one to pray to but you. The star nations all over the heavens are yours, and yours are the grasses of the earth. You are older than all need, older than all pain and prayer. Grandfather, Great Spirit, fill us with the light. Give us the strength to understand and the eyes to see. Teach us to walk the soft earth as relatives to all that live. Help us, for without you we are nothing.

LUTHER STANDING BEAR, LAKOTA-SIOUX PEOPLES.

Brendan's Return Voyage: A New American Dream

THERE ARE MORE THAN a thousand indigenous tribes or First Nation Peoples. Many of them are in Australasia. Over three million live in USA and Canada. The Creator's imprint is in the DNA of each of them.

> "We are all flowers in the Great Spirit's garden. We share a common root, and the root is Mother Earth". Hopi Prophecy.

> *"The person who blesses themselves in the earth shall find themselves in the God of Truth."* Jeremiah 4:2.

Virtually all indigenous tribes know that the plants and creatures are not inert objects to be misused for their own selfish purposes. They are to be treated like brothers and sisters. They reflect the advice God gave to Job in the Bible: *"Ask the animals and they will teach you"* (Job 12:7–10). Chief Seattle, of the Suquamish tribe, said "What are humans without the animals? If all the animals were gone humans would die of loneliness of spirit". Luther Standing Bear, an Oglala Lakota chief and educator who died in 1935, taught that "From the Great Spirit . . . there came a great unifying life force that flowed in and through all things—the flowers of the plains, blowing winds, rocks, trees, birds, animals—and was the same force that had been breathed into the first man. Thus all things were kindred and were brought together by the same Great Mystery. Reflecting back, he said that the world was a library and its books were the stones, leaves, grass, brooks, and the birds and animals that shared, alike with us, the storms and blessings of earth."

The Bible teaches that Jesus descended to the lower parts of the earth—he, too, is deeply connected to the earth. The first human being is named Adam because he is created from adamah (earth), and Genesis 1:8 makes considerable play of the bond between them, for Adam is estranged from the earth through his disobedience. The Bible speaks of Jesus as The Second or Ultimate Earth Man, 1 Corinthians 15:45.

Many tribal ceremonies are connected to the earth, as are prayers such as this:

> Earth teach me stillness as the grasses are stilled with light.
> Earth teach me suffering as old stones suffer with memory.
> Earth teach me humility as blossoms are humble with beginning.
> Earth teach me caring as the mother who secures her young.
> Earth teach me courage as the tree which stands alone.
> Earth teach me limitation as the ant which crawls on the ground.
> Earth teach me freedom as the eagle which soars in the sky.
> Earth teach me resignation as the leaves which die in the fall.

Earth teach me regeneration as the seed which rises in the spring.
Earth teach me to forget myself as melted snow forgets its life
Ute tribe

The fact that the tribes also have a relationship with what grows upon the earth is another sign of the Creator's imprint within them. They let trees and skies speak to them. The Creator spoke to Moses through a bush, to Jeremiah through an almond tree, to astrologers through a star and He continues to speak to his tribes in such ways. The Bible begins with a tree of life, the psalms speak of trees that clap their hands, and trees feature in the vision of the new creation with which the Bible ends. The leaves of one of these trees are for the healing of the tribes. Hopi people use the sap of the pinyon pine as an anti-biotic for a wound.

In February Hopi women do a bean dance. They call these beans their children. They plant and nurture them. If these "children" grow well it is a sign to the tribe that their whole season will be blessed.

Another imprint is the elders. The elders are honored within the tribal relationship: they are not marginalized because they have no utilitarian value. The remembering and honoring of ancestors is another imprint of the Creator, reminiscent of the "great cloud of witnesses" mentioned in Hebrews chapter 12. *"Honor all people"* 1 Peter 2:17.

The power of silence and therefore the power of mindful words are also valued. *"Let a person sit alone in silence"* Lamentation 3:28.

For three decades a white American named Kent Nerburn took a job on the Red Lake Ojibwe reservation in the pine forests of northern Minnesota. He had sensitivity and the humility to learn from the indigenous people. His many books, such as *Wisdom of the Native Americans* (New World Library 1999) have helped to bridge the gap between western Judeo-Christian and Native traditions.

He helps us to see that the task of humans is not to dominate but to understand; to learn the rules of the universe and come into right relationship with them. Only then will the Creator's favor be upon them and the powers of the world be at their command. He warns that when we lose the heart to be listeners and learners, without thinking we reduce the world around us to a series of objects. We do not see the "thou" in our fellow creatures, only the "it". We forget that all human beings reflect something of God's image, Genesis 1:26.

He recognizes that the Native people feel a deep spiritual yearning; they understand religion as a cast of mind rather than as a list of doctrines.

Like Taoism it understands ourselves as part of nature. The Native way says "Look to the tree as a lesson in praise, because it holds its arms to the sky, even in the most powerful storm. Learn humility in the face of success from the turning of the seasons. Learn watchfulness from the wolf, faithfulness from the dog, different ways of parenting from the oriole and the eagle". *"Learn from the ant and be wise"* says Proverbs 6:6.

This is illustrated in an email to me from a white American minister: "Our First Nation cousins hold a remembrance ritual for the "Dakota 38" in Mankato, MN. It is solemn and highly spiritual. Following the US-Dakota (people) War of 1862, 38 men were hanged for their "war crimes." It was and remains highly controversial; the story is much longer. Dakota people gather every December 26th to remember and honor. Runners start at the hated Fort Snelling while riders start from the west for a multiple day and difficult journey. The ceremonies start when they arrive. Two happenings touched me deeply.

The first was the passing of "leadership" from one medicine man to the next. The then-current leader talked about how the mantle should be passed on not by virtue of intellect but by spirit. The leader talked about how he prayed and purified himself in preparation for a vision of who should come next. It was pure seeking after God/Great Spirit. He agonized over the decision until it was made clear to him who should come next. The next gentleman hadn't a clue, it was not a position to be sought after. The handing over of a staff involved much prayer and honor. It was all about leadership passed on through spiritual discernment."

Another sign of the Creator's imprint is the indigenous peoples' attitude towards the land. The Bible teaches that the land belongs to God: *"The earth is the Lord's"* Psalm 24:1. Humans cannot own it. If they have purchase agreements according to their local man-made laws, these should be seen as custodian agreements. A member of the Community of Aidan and Hilda in Australia has given back bush land she inherited from her "land grab" grandparents, to be common land used in perpetuity for those who wish to enjoy it. She has put up a notice honoring the tribes who used to be its custodians, welcoming them back. On the properties where her family lives she describes them, too, as custodians.

The Cherokee believe that stories and ceremonies help the people to stay in balance. They attribute their survival to Duyukta –which means the path of being in balance. *"There is an appointed time for everything"* Ecclesiastes 3:1.

An old Cherokee was teaching his grandson about life. "A fight is going on inside me," he said to the boy. "It is a terrible fight and it is between two wolves. One is evil—he is anger, envy, sorrow, regret, greed, arrogance, self-pity, guilt, resentment, inferiority, lies, false pride, superiority, and ego." He continued, "The other is good—he is joy, peace, love, hope, serenity, humility, kindness, benevolence, empathy, generosity, truth, compassion, and faith. The same fight is going on inside you—and inside every other person, too." The grandson thought about it for a minute and then asked his grandfather, "Which wolf will win?" The old Cherokee simply replied, "The one you feed." These insights reflect the New Testament teachings about the fruits of the carnal life and the fruits of the Spirit, Galatians 5:19–26.

Randy Woodley, a Keetoowah Cherokee, and, when I met him, director of intercultural studies at George Fox Seminary, Portland, did extensive Ph.D. research on indigenous beliefs, and asked himself if there was any common thread that he could make into a construct. He concluded that there were enough parallel insights for him to create a construct which he calls The Harmony Way, and which he compares to the biblical understanding of Shalom. He has heard of similar testimonies of a type of harmony way of living from Zulu, Inca, Maasai, Sami, Maori, Inuit, Australian Aboriginal, and Hawaiian as well as from USA Indian people. He concludes that the ancient Semitic shalom construct, or what we can broadly refer to as the Harmony Way, is the Creator's original instruction for the way in which all societies should be ordered, and for how all life on this planet should be lived . . . Shalom is not a utopian construct, it is a constant journey . . . This active, persistent effort takes place at every level, from personal relationships to societal and structural transformation . . . Jesus . . . coming into the world from the shalom of the Trinity is the intention of God's mission of birthing and restoring shalom to the world. Woodley quotes Old Testament scholar Walter Brueggemann: The central vision of world history in the Bible is that all creation is one, every creature in community with every other, living in harmony and security toward the joy and well-being of every other creature.[1]

A rain dance ceremony of the Athaspascan-Navajo tellingly captures this:

---

1. Eerdmans, *Shalom*, 19.

As I walk, as I walk
The universe is walking with me.
Beautifully—it walks before me.
Beautifully—it walks behind me.
Beautifully—it walks below me.
Beautifully—it walks above me.
Beautifully—on every side
As I walk—as I walk with Beauty.

Many tribes are named in the Bible. They have some one hundred names for God. These names sometimes describe a characteristic of the divine or an encounter that occurred in a particular place. For example, Jehovah Jireh means "The Lord will provide" because he provided Abraham with a lamb in that place (Genesis 22:14). El comes from a root word meaning strength or power. Elohim can mean The Powers. The tribes recognize Powers. El Roi can mean The Seeing One. Shalom (Judges 6), The Name of God is Harmony. YHWH can mean "I am what I am". Aravat (or Avarat)—Father of Creation, is mentioned once in 2 Enoch. Bore means The Creator. HaRachaman is The Merciful One. Malbish Arumim is Clother of the Naked. Matir Asurim is Freer of the Captives. Mechayeh HaKol is Life giver to All. Pokeach Ivrim means Opener of Blind Eyes, Rofeh Cholim, Healer of the Sick. Shomer Yisrael—is Guardian of Israel (Psalm 121:4). Somech Noflim is Supporter of the Fallen. Uri Gol is The New LORD for a New Era (Judges 5:14). Yotsehr Or means Fashioner of Light and Zokef Kefufim means Straightener of the Bent. The Indian tribes have similar names and add to this rich menu.

At first Moses knew God only by his tribal name. When he had to go to Egypt he asked to be shown the new name for God that he should use. Why should such experiences be confined to one tribe? Sometimes a god name embraces both good and evil, a view reflected in Isaiah 45:7: "*I make peace and create evil*" KJV. Hopis use the name Masau. This can mean "where it all begins" or "The One who looks after all things and tells us what to do". I was told that Masau can also mean "One Who is false and tells you lies". God has implanted a knowledge of good and evil in all his tribes. Some Hopis make sense of this by saying that there are two Masaus: one is good and the other is false. Thus, the truth behind the biblical portrayal of a devil and of demons is also imprinted in tribal DNA. Yet another teaching is that Masau is the "living death spirit". He has blood on his facial mask. After his death he comes to life again.

I was shown an 800 years old painting of a significant figure in a now extinct tribe. This chief had no spear, he had feathers, a symbol of prayer. His authority was shown by tears falling down his cheeks. This teaches us that authority comes from the heart and is about relationship—surely an imprint of Jesus.

Many tribes have a story about something in their heritage which will be made complete sometime in the future. One tribe has a tradition that there are two halves of a tablet. The first half, engraved with truths, is in the custody of their elders. The second half will be brought by someone from the east at an unknown time. Wisdom acknowledges incompleteness and welcomes the One who comes to fulfill what is lacking.

The circle and the cross is a hallowed symbol among Christians in Celtic and other lands. Lakota Medicine Man Black Elk said . . .

> "You have noticed that everything an Indian does is in a circle, and this is because the Power of the World always works in circles, and everything tries to be round.
>
> In the old days when we were a strong and happy people, all our power came to us from the sacred hoop of the nation, and so long as the hoop was unbroken, the people flourished. The flowering tree was the living center of the hoop, and the circle of the four quarters nourished it. The east gave peace and light, the south gave warmth, the west gave rain, and the north with its cold and mighty wind gave strength and endurance. This knowledge came to us from the outer world with our religion.
>
> Everything the Power of the World does is done in a circle. The sky is round, and I have heard that the earth is round like a ball, and so are all the stars. The wind, in its greatest power, whirls. Birds make their nests in circles, for theirs is the same religion as ours.
>
> The sun comes forth and goes down again in a circle. The moon does the same, and both are round. Even the seasons form a great circle in their changing, and always come back again to where they were.
>
> The life of a man (sic) is a circle from childhood to childhood, and so it is in everything where power moves. Our tepees were round like the nests of birds, and these were always set in a circle, the nation's hoop, a nest of many nests, where the Great Spirit meant for us to hatch our children".[2]

The psalms refer to an assembly of the gods and John refers to the spirits which we must test (1 John 4:4). Adonai means the Lord of lords

2. Raven, 'The Wheel.

(Deuteronomy 10:17). In the Katsina dance ceremonies in Pueblo tribes, men wear masks to represent the spirits. Hopis give their prayers to the boys who pass them on to the Katsinas. One Hopi told me that they pass them on to some higher authority, or Creator. Jesus's followers can ask in their hearts that they will be passed to Jesus. Certain Protestant missionaries condemn this practice. They also condemn Catholics for praying to saints. But Catholics say they are asking the saints to pass on their prayers to God. The Hopis can do something similar. If Jesus the Pantocrator has created a rich diversity of beings, who are we to so proudly ignore them? Protestants who tell Indians to ditch all ceremonies that involve spirits fail to heed that New Testament advice to exercise discernment of spirits (1 John 4:1; 1 Corinthians 12:10). Nita, a Hopi who follows Jesus, wondered whether she could go back to her kiva to pray among her own people. The Holy Spirit put into her mind a picture of a shopping mall. One can walk down the mall, but that does not mean that you believe in the products sold in every single store.[3] *"To the pure all things are pure"* (Titus 1:15). Some white missionaries tell natives to repent of their spirits, but they don't tell the white churches to repent of the spirit of consumerism.

When a tribe learns about Jesus it is good if they ask him to show them which spirits are good and to deliver them from bad spirits, it is not good to be closed to the spirit world. When God spoke to me at midnight one New Year on Britain's Holy Island of Lindisfarne he told me he wanted western Christians to restore the connection with the unseen world which they had lost. The tribes have not lost this connection.

Millie Toms realized, as a missionary from a non-Native culture, that it is not up to cultural outsiders to determine what is redeemable; it is up to each Native believer to discern what is acceptable for them. She knows someone who is a "holy water carrier" in a very traditional village, who believes she should continue to bring water to her people for their dances and ceremonies because this is where she can pray for them to know Jesus as she does. Hopi people put eaglets on their roof, kill them in summer and use their feathers to adorn their prayer sticks. These are believed to carry their prayers to the Creator. People like Millie pray that these birds will be spared as Hopis come to realize that the ultimate sacrifice has been paid by Jesus on the cross.

Similarly with symbols. In Scripture some animals can symbolize both a negative and a positive quality. In the story of the Garden of Eden

3. Ehn-Toms, *Great Eagle Rising.*

the snake is a slimy temptress. In the story of Moses and the bronze serpent it becomes a symbol of authority to which Christ likened himself.

Anthropologists Andrew Lang and Wilhelm Schmidt wrote twelve volumes which confirm that monotheist beliefs existed from earliest time.[4]

Many Indian tribes speak of The Great Spirit:

> O Great Spirit whose voice I hear in the winds
> And whose breath gives life to all the world . . .
> Let me walk in beauty, and make my eyes ever behold the red and
> purple sunset.
> Make my hands respect the things you have made and my ears
> sharp to hear your voice.
> Make me wise so that I may understand the things you have taught
> my people.
> Let me learn the lessons you have hidden in every leaf and rock.
> I seek strength, not to be greater than my brother,
> but to fight my greatest enemy—myself.
> Make me always ready to come to you with clean hands and
> straight eyes.
> So when life fades, as the fading sunset, my spirit may come to you
> without shame.
> Translated by Lakota Sioux Chief Yellow Lark in 1887.

YWAM has a CALL school (College of Acquiring Language & Linguistics) centered in Flagstaff and the Hopi reservation. They teach "Uni-Skript" which uses indigenous cultural symbols to create unique native alphabets. It has been successfully done with the Navajo. It plans to recruit Hopi believer friends to become the language informants and eventually the paid instructors. The Hopis have only a New Testament but now have a plan to tackle the small book of Ruth. Some students come from all over for a 2 weeks Masters course. The goal is to eventually focus translation efforts on the many Pacific Island nations, that have no Bibles.

Nerburn[5] wrote that arrogance was foreign to native teaching; speech is a perilous gift; silence is a sign of perfect equilibrium. Some Hopis believe that in order to stay quiet and gentle for the earth's recovery you must put ashes on your forehead to protect you from spirits who might otherwise take away your breath. This is surely the same principle that mindfulness trainers use—they suggest tools that help us to concentrate on our breathing.

---

4. Schmidt and Bornemann, *Der Ursprung der Gottesidee* (also, *The Origin and Growth,* Schmidt *High Gods*)

5. Nerburn, *Voices in the Stones* 7–8

The Navajo have a concept called Hozho. This can mean "walking in beauty or harmony". If a person gets out of harmony, ceremonial songs and paintings are used that help to restore them to harmony. To the Palute people a feather represents a messenger or warning, a snake skin represents wisdom. We all need reminders of the value of warnings and wisdom.

Another imprint of the Creator in these cultures is hospitality. Those who have food consider it their sacred duty to share their food with those who are hungry. At a chief's funeral all his possessions were given to mourners. A struggling Lakota family spent all its money to provide a feast for mourners for the entire community when a family member died. *"By showing hospitality some have entertained angels without realizing it"* Hebrews 13:2. Father Chrestian Leclerq, a seventeenth century Jesuit missionary, wrote that hospitality is in such great esteem among the Mi'kmaq people that they make almost no distinction between the home-born and the stranger. They give lodging equally to the French and to the Indians who come from a distance, and to both they distribute generously whatever they have obtained in hunting and fishing.[6] This stems from a sense of inter-connectedness. The Lakota people often say "We're all relations". The Menomini tribe, like many others, include all their children as participants, whatever the inconvenience. The Inuit people of Northern Canada create a life-like rock figure placed as a direction sign for travelers and to remind them that we are not alone. Christopher Jocks tells how his Mohawk friend illustrates the hospitality inherent in an Indian ceremony: First you cook up lots and lots of food. As you are cooking it, think about the people you'll be inviting. Think about where the ingredients come from and who helped bring them to you. Then invite everyone you know to come over. Everybody who comes, you feed them. Then listen to them, pay attention to their advice, their problems. Hold their hands, if that's what they need. If any of them needs to stay over, make a place for them. Then, next month, you do the same thing again. And again, four times, the same way. That's it. You've done an Indian ceremony.

Imprints of the Creator can also be seen in the Indians role as co-creators, a role which is often forgotten in modern times. Before the Great Drought of the twelfth and thirteenth centuries, the genocides attempted by white settlers following Columbus' arrival in 1492 and the Great Plagues of the sixteenth century Indian peoples in Oregon alone sustained

---

6. Lowe, *Indigenous Hospitality* 47–59

civilizations that had observatories, canals, an early form of solar heating and micro-agriculture that fed 80,000 people.

In the Bible there are many prophets. Most of them are false but a few are true. Indigenous peoples also have prophets of both kinds. According to legend, Shining Shirt, a chief and shaman of the Kalispel tribe, prophesied that white men would come from the east one day. A Power told him that there were a Good One and an Evil One of which the Indian so far knew little: the white men would tell them about them.

The Bible tells of many tribes. Twelve of them came from one chief who had great faults but was determined to overcome every obstacle. These tribes not only fought other tribes, they fought between themselves. Despite this the Creator found ways of teaching and preparing them. North America's tribes were usually more peaceful; they were content with their own land and did not colonize. When western colonizers arrived they often welcomed them and gave them food. This turned sour when the western people mistreated and attacked them. Western Christians who then built mission stations so that Indians would accept their Jesus as their Savior made two terrible mistakes. The first mistake was that they did not look for signs of the Creator in the tribes. The second mistake was that they told indigenous converts that in order to follow Jesus they had to accept the missionaries' culture and throw away their culture as rubbish. This has created confusion in churches to this day as to the nature of Jesus: to many he is the white man's god.

The missionaries were blinded by pride. They assumed their own culture was Christian and the indigenous culture was godless. The truth was that the missionaries needed to repent for the rubbish in their own culture, discern what was of God in indigenous culture, and journey with the tribe's Jesus welcomers, asking Jesus to reveal himself in their ceremonies, music, art, dance, customs, and aspirations and to journey together with Jesus to heal the bad things in both First Nation and Western cultures.

Many tribal ceremonies involve music, dancing, and wearing of masks. King David danced naked before the Lord and his wife was rebuked for condemning him for this. A white missionary felt God rebuke her for her wrong attitude to someone dancing.

Incense is used in the Old Testament temple and in the new heaven and earth envisaged in the Book of Revelation. Some tribes use leaves and berries to make incense. Many create smoke for smudging—as the smoke is

15

wafted to each part of the body it receives cleansing. This is a humble thing to do. It is a constant reminder that we need cleansing.

My friend Casey Church, director of the Wiconi ministry to Native American and First Nations people, who comes from the Potawatomi people, identifies four indigenous customs that he uses in Christian worship. The first is the use of smoke or incense as a symbol of cleansing; the second is the use of drums with worship songs; the third is the use of pipes and dance; and the fourth is the sweat lodge ceremony. He lights a candle as the group sits in the sweat lodge, and invites the Holy Spirit to help them relax, trust and enjoy friendship as they share their stories.[7]

Although this is better than a blanket dismissal of all native ceremonies, other Christians involved in native ministries think it is important that elders and members of each tribe continue their own communal ceremonies but ask Jesus to show them what is good and change what is bad in them. Otherwise the church undermines community. Those who adopt that approach listen to and learn from one another, honor the past, invite Jesus to heal hurts, and share inspirations as they journey.

Some Protestant missionaries dismiss such understandings as these with the words "you can only be saved by the name of Jesus". But in Hawaiian and other native languages you don't say "What is your name?" but "Who is your name?" Yeshua, (translated into English as Jesus) is related to Yahweh (I Am): his name means God saves. Who saves people in any tribe? The god who saves, the god who is.

Randy Woodley[8] tells how a church he planted in Nevada only really "became native" when the non-natives gave up leadership. From that time, they arranged the chairs in a circle and changed from being a church that did a lot of native things to being a native church. When I stayed with the Woodleys on their farm I felt God say "Take off your shoes, listen, for you are on holy ground".

Sometimes the Creator's imprints seem to be destroyed, but a person of courage and vision retrieves from the rubbish dump, pearls of great price. Such people may be likened to Queen Esther, in the Old Testament; she remained true to the ways of her people although she was exiled from them in a foreign land. A native figurehead who remained true to the native vision despite being railroaded by colonial incomers is Ohijesa, also known by his Anglicized name Charles Alexander Eastman. He came from the

7. Church, *His Holy Smoke*
8. Woodley, *Living in Color*, 47

Dakota (Sioux) nation in southern Minnesota where he was born in 1858. He witnessed the massacre of many of his people. His father was incarcerated by white men, but later returned to his son, convinced that the native way of life could not survive the European invasion, and despising "reservation Indians" who lived on hand-outs from the whites. He took his son to a small plot of farming land in South Dakota, sent him to a white school, and taught him to be a warrior within this new context. Ohijesa studied at universities, practiced as a doctor, and devoted himself to bringing the voice of the Indian into American intellectual life. He became involved in the Boy Scout movement and set up a camp in New Hampshire which tried to give non-Indian boys a taste of Sioux education and values. In his auto-biography[9] he strove to help Americans find a shared vision, rooted in the values he held within himself. He followed, as his grandmother had advised, a new trail. He accepted the passing of the old Indian structures as the workings of the Great Mystery and was open to explore "the Christ Ideal". In his writings he described how Indians valued justice, honesty, friendship, generosity and bravery. He upheld the role they gave to prophets, and told of those who had prophesied the coming of white men fifty years ahead of the first arrivals.

If Ohijesa was some type of Esther figure, most Indians were not. Many Indians of mixed blood who have left reservations have been unable to reconcile within themselves the two world views. They are angry, tormented figures. We should listen to their anger.

Steven Charleston, both a Chocktaw Indian and a Christian bishop, is an example of someone who has been able to reconcile two worlds. In his book *The Four Vision Quests of Jesus*[10] he sees resonances between native and biblical traditions. For example, the *koshares* of the South West and the *heyokas* of the plains are clown figures who are spiritual teachers. Other native traditions feature the trickster. In dances their role may be provocative. They help people do things opposite ways to what is normal. In this respect they are akin to prophets like John the Baptist who shook people out of their familiar comfort zones until they saw truth from a new angle. They challenge people to be open to another dimension. They embody spiritual mindfulness. John the Baptist, argues Charleston, is a similar figure; by showing people how bad things can be he prepares them for how good they can be through Jesus.

9. Eastman, *Deep Woods*
10. Charleston, *Four Vision*

The Native Covenant is inclusive: there is kinship with people of diverse backgrounds. God is the author of diversity and therefore diversity is holy. When Jesus issues his manifesto he announces good news for the poor and release for the prisoner, and freeing of people from debts. Both John and Jesus risk rejection in order to give themselves away for the good of the people. This giving away, which includes hospitality, speaks to Native spirituality. Charleston calls this give-away theology.

Charleston tells the story of the Indian woman Pocahontas. She was the Indian Princess who saved Captain John Smith from death at the hands of her father. She became an Imperial Princess who numbers two First Ladies among her descendants, the wives of Theodore Roosevelt and Ronald Reagan. Charleston asks whether the painting in the Capitol building of this Indian woman being baptized is mere window dressing for white racism, or is a fulfillment of the native peoples' own covenant with God? The hypocrisy of idolizing Pocahontas while murdering her sisters was obvious. Through reflecting deeply on the four vision quests of Jesus—the wilderness, the mountain, the garden, and the cross—he eventually came to the conclusion that a Native American can embrace the New Covenant of the Native Messiah, not as a mask for European colonialism, but as an authentic expression of their own liberation.

No two people are the same, and God starts from where we are. Many people in reservations suffer from alcohol, drugs or sexual abuse, but God anoints children of the Messiah who will exchange "beauty instead of ashes, the mantle of praise instead of a faint spirit" (Isaiah 61:3). The covenant promise of God applies to these adopted children that *"You shall no more be termed Forsaken but you shall be termed, My Delight is in Her and your land Married"* (Isaiah 62:4).

Much of indigenous spirituality exists on the edges of society without validation or integration from the government and popular culture (though it is often appropriated for commercial or selfish purposes). Native lands were largely invaded by Christian colonizers. Native peoples were forced to leave their homes. Their children were taken to schools where their culture was often stripped away.

From this marginalized position, Native peoples have a unique "bias from the bottom" that we would do well to pay attention to. We could learn from them, among other things, that land cannot be owned and Spirit cannot be divided. The Earth and all its inhabitants belong to the Creator who made them. We are called to live in harmony with each other and all created things.

Huston Smith described "primal peoples" as:

> ... oriented to a single cosmos, which sustains them like a living womb. Because they assume that it exists to nurture them, they have no disposition to challenge it, defy it, refashion it, or escape from it. It is not a place of exile or pilgrimage, though pilgrimages take place within it. Its space is not homogenous; the home has a number of rooms, we might say, some of which are normally invisible. But together they constitute a single domicile. Primal peoples are concerned with the maintenance of personal, social, and cosmic harmony. But the overriding goal of salvation that dominates the historical religions is virtually absent from them.[11]

When Pope John Paul II met with Native Americans in Phoenix, Arizona, he told them

> "Your ancestors' ways were marked by great respect for the natural resources of land and rivers, of forest and plain, and desert. ... Here they worshipped the Creator and thanked him for his gifts. In contact with the forces of nature they learned the value of prayer, of silence and fasting, of patience and courage in the face of pain and disappointment."[12]

It would be wrong to over romanticize America's indigenous tribes. But not to recognize the imprint of the Creator among them would be a far more heinous wrong.

11. Smith, *World's Religions*, 377.

12. *Pope John Paul II, Address to Native Peoples.*

3

What's Wrong and What's Right
with the West?

NATIONS, LIKE PERSONS, ARE ego-centric. All people tend to presume that the culture they are reared in is the norm. They assume it is better than others and try to fit everyone else into their construct. Ancient Chinese dynasties published maps of the world with China colored pink in the center and the rest of the world labeled as barbarians around the edge. The European empires, and now what the rest of the world thinks of as the American empire, have followed this pattern.

One thousand years ago America was home to an ancient civilization. Some five hundred years later settlers began to arrive from Europe. They regarded everything as frontier. They came to build from scratch. In 1803 Thomas Jefferson purchased a vast tract of land in the west from the French, ignoring the fact that First Nation peoples already claimed it. The settlers saw this as their "Manifest Destiny". Over 400,000 trekked West. In 1862 the Homestead Act allowed these cowboys to settle. They came with the gun culture—hence the 'Cowboys and Indians' battles that have filled countless film screens.

The gun culture was birthed in the 1770's War of Independence from the British colonial power and was enshrined in the Right to Bear Arms Act of 1791. From the 1860's endless indigenous peoples were shot, and those who survived the guns were herded into reservations, where high levels of depression, poverty and mental illness ensued.

Bloodshed became central to American identity. Her first president, George Washington, was chosen because of his military prowess. The settlers projected an image of themselves as akin to the biblical Israelites coming to the promised land, and they projected the indigenous peoples as akin to godless Canaanite tribes. The settlers neglected the great biblical prophets: for example, Jeremiah's accusation that the people were like whores. They had married power, sex and money to their god; they had neglected Yahweh's priorities of truth, justice and mercy. As a result the earth suffered and would become sterile (Jeremiah 3 and 4). The settlers married conquest, sex and money-making to America, its flag and its God.

The Old Testament is the most honest of the world's scriptures. It admits that Israel became arrogant and turned to false gods, that it forfeited God's favor and was thus overruled and exiled; that it had got its image of its messiah wrong. The messiah would be a suffering servant and make a way for all nations to receive the light.

Walter Brueggemann begins his classic work *The Prophetic Imagination* with this statement:

> "The contemporary American church is so largely enculturated
> to the American ethos of consumerism that it has little power to
> believe or to act. This enculturation is in some way true across the
> spectrum of church life, both liberal and conservative."[1]

James C. Scott[2] talks about public transcripts that those with power tell to ensure that people see the world their way. These are the transcripts that explain why some deserve to flourish and others do not. People who invade tell stories to justify to themselves why they—as good people, and we all want to be good people—can do this. Scott also talks of hidden transcripts—the stories that oppressed people tell in private to sustain their lives. They are stories that mock those with power and affirm their own worth. They are dangerous stories, and when they surface in public spaces they are often ambiguous stories—i.e. stories that seem harmless to those with power, but are understood as quite subversive by those with ears to hear.

Scott suggests that this dynamic was at play in the story of Jesus and taxes (Mark 12:13–17). The story starts with people coming to Jesus to trap him. They ask Jesus is it ok to pay taxes to the Romans? Romans didn't pay taxes; only those who were defeated militarily. Taxes were a constant reminder of occupation. Jesus asks the religious leaders for a coin, which they produce fairly quickly. The coin had the emperor on one side and his

1. Brueggemann, *Prophetic Imagination*
2. Scott, *Dominion*

mother—claimed to be a deity—on the other. This was a first-class example of idolatry, and yet they used the coin. It takes away their high moral ground. Jesus looks at the coin and says: give to Caesar what is Caesar's and to God what is God's. Good answer –it affirms the Romans and God—and Jesus is safe. But while this interpretation suits us, it is—I think—fundamentally wrong. Jesus believes that everything belongs to God. In Jesus' world there is nothing left for Caesar and his idolatrous claims. And those who knew Jesus heard this as a word of hope.

Post-colonial theology explicitly recognizes the way narratives and celebrations support or question power and it seeks to take the side of those who are oppressed and marginalized. It is a form of theology that is closer to a hidden transcript. Postcolonial theology also stands against the way our society has, for three hundred years, divided the world into religious, political, and economic spheres. It claims that religion is not a separate part of life but is deeply woven into every part of daily life. Religion is not just about personal and individual beliefs and behaviour. It is the narrative that holds together, underpins and makes sense of the world. It is a communally agreed set of social practices and rituals. The problem when we let the world be divided into spheres is, (i) religion is told to leave politics and economics alone and (ii) these other two areas of life have their own narrative and story of salvation—"security" for the state and "the market" for the economy.

Postcolonial theology helps us face up to the truth. It reminds us that sin is not just personal and between us and God, though it is that. It is also communal; it destroys and fractures our common life and makes peoples' relationship with God quite unhealthy. Some modern theologies are so busy escaping the distorted emphasis on fall and sin that has marked Protestant theology, that they find it hard to name evil and wrong-doing. But we need a theology that encourages truth-telling, acknowledgement/confession, reparation and, hopefully at some point, forgiveness.

From a white western perspective America "was founded upon the belief that this country was bringing about a new birth for humanity, and that America, born out of a decadent European world, was the last great hope of the human community."[3] From an indigenous perspective the USA is the story of plunder.

3. Berry, *Sacred Universe.*

The Twin Towers of What Is Wrong with America

Christ confirms what is good and corrects what is bad in every culture. So much is good about America, but before we look at that, let us identify what are the twin towers of what is rotten in the Western world-view of which USA is the showpiece.

My heart froze when I saw TV pictures of the Twin Towers catastrophe: it melted when I heard the sobbing voice of a young American "Will someone please tell me why the world hates Americans?" When we become vulnerable, people love us. I love Americans, but I know that question deserves the most profound answer. The answer must be based on radical reflection and should not undermine what is noble in America.

The twin towers of what is rotten in the Western world view of which the USA is the showpiece are godless but are perceived to be godly, which makes them as difficult to remove as the Pharisaic Tendency was difficult for Jesus to remove. The first twin tower is Empire building, harnessed to competition and the worship of money, in the name of "manifest destiny", self-improvement and the "rags to riches" dream. The second twin tower is Separation—separation of business from ethics, society from Christ, creation from God.

Empire-Building Disguised as Manifest Destiny

The first tower of empire building consists of the three things Jesus was tempted to put first during his wilderness testing: to find his identity in what he possessed, in what he did, and in what others thought of him. In order to climb the "rags to riches" ladder we have to push others out of our way. It becomes a competition for the survival of the fittest. If we are climbing a ladder we separate ourselves from everyone else. Even church-goers become competitive. Community has no place on a ladder.

Western peoples have brought industry and technology to the world but they have also trampled on it. The drive to explore, produce, and organize can be harnessed to co-operation with the humans and creatures with whom we share our common home. In America, however (and before that in the European empires) this drive insensibly fell prey to the empire-building virus that Jesus warned us against, (Matthew 20:25–28). Western settlers treated the indigenous tribes badly. Even when their missionaries came to tell them about the most wonderful Person, too many of them failed to cherish the imprints of Jesus in their culture. To separate Jesus from their culture and require them to adopt western culture if they wished to follow Jesus was a terrible form of abuse. To lie to them about keeping treaties and to massacre them when some of them resisted abuses was a crime against heaven.

Capitalism began with the assumption that a free money market would not displace families and local working communities whose care for their members would continue regardless of their cash value. Soon, however, it made competition-for-cash its god rather than its servant. Jesus' warning that *"you cannot serve God and money"* was ignored (Luke 16:13). Envy took root like a weed and competition became a blood sport. Silicon Valley chiefs have created internet platforms without moral values or account-ability frameworks. This has undermined millions of parents who do take responsibility. The opposite of competition is not lethargy and mediocrity, it is rising to our full stature in relationship to others and the earth.

The drive to invent, build, organize and distribute has brought un-doubted and wide-spread material benefits, but to do these things without regard to the earth which sustains us and the human community of which we are part is not good. Capitalism has put material "success" above values. Mi'kmaq historian Daniel N. Paul explains:

> Throughout their history Europeans have tended to equate civi-lization with the tools of technology and war rather than with human values. The ability to invent a tool that efficiently killed or disabled came to be seen as the mark of civilization. The tenacity of Native Americans in refusing to accept these foreign models of "civilization", and to fight to preserve their cultures and life-styles, was probably for European leaders the most frustrating of their colonial experience. This frustration was compounded when the observation was made by some of their own intellectuals that cer-tain social values inherent in Native civilizations were superior to their own.[4]

Growth as god leads to a dead end. America's policy of unlimited economic growth is unsustainable since the planet has limited resources, perhaps began with its voracious appetite for native land. Its growth is built upon debt, a staggering 8 trillion dollars. Ray Dalio, the billionaire chairman of the investment firm Bridgewater Associates warned in April 2019 that

---

4. Paul, *We were not the Savages.*

America faced a national emergency: its manic hyper-capitalism's failure to benefit more people, and he pronounced the American Dream lost.

Growth as god treats indigenous people as rubbish. Indigenous peoples understand this. So many have been abused by colonial people (as well as by one another), so many have sunk into addictions and despair that they dismiss the West, except for its technology, as alien and harmful. Mark Charles, a Navajo believer and activist who speaks and lectures throughout the country regarding American Indian social justice issues, points out that the Declaration of Independence refers to Native Americans as "merciless Indian Savages". Others describe how settlers deliberately created dependency so that tribes had to pay their debts by ceding lands. The US honors President Andrew Jackson as a nation-builder who drove westward expansion; his image is placed on the $20 bill. Yet it was he who in the 1830s promoted "Indian removal", the banishment of Native Americans from their ancestral homelands, their enforced relocation on desolate reservations, and who oversaw the infamous Trail of Tears, the forced migration during which more than 20 percent of the Cherokee people perished.

Growth-as-god even terminated some indigenous tribes: from the mid-1940s to the mid-1960s it was federal policy to terminate independent Indian tribes. The belief was that indigenous people should abandon their traditional lives and begin to live as (White) Americans. Congress set about ending the special relationship between tribes and the federal government, including the rights of reservations, and to make all native persons become taxpaying citizens, subject to state and federal taxes as well as laws, from which they had previously been exempt. From the native standpoint, Northern Cheyenne former U.S. Senator from Colorado Ben Nighthorse Campbell said of assimilation and termination in a speech delivered in Montana:

> "If you can't change them, absorb them until they simply disappear into the mainstream culture . . . In Washington's infinite wisdom, it was decided that tribes should no longer be tribes, never mind that they had been tribes for thousands of years."

I have found accounts of the endless atrocities committed against America's indigenous tribes almost unbearable to read. Such blasphemy against the image of God in these people seems only explicable if the perpetrators created a self-justifying narrative.

One indigenous lecturer, Randy Woodley, portrays this selfish, consumer-driven mentality that values wealth and gain over justice and peace as the false premise of the American Dream. He argues that the United

States, although originally composed of many individuals who claimed to be Christians, was in fact never built on purely Christian principles.

This false premise was cloaked in two grand deceptions. The first was "The Doctrine of Discovery", and the second was the doctrine of Manifest Destiny. The Doctrine of Discovery was contained in a series of Papal Bulls (official edicts) written in the fifteenth century. The Papal Bull Inter Caeter, issued by Pope Alexander VI on May 4, 1493, played a central role in the Spanish conquest of the New World. The document supported Spain's strategy to ensure its exclusive right to the lands discovered by Columbus the previous year. Mark Charles summarizes the Doctrine in this way: "The Doctrine of Discovery is the Church in Europe saying to the nations of Europe, whatever lands you find not ruled by Christian rulers, those people are less than human and their lands are yours for the taking." Charles goes on to say, "It was the Doctrine of Discovery that justified European nations colonizing Africa and enslaving the African people. It was also the Doctrine of Discovery that allowed Christopher Columbus to get lost at sea, land in a new world that was already inhabited by millions and claim to have "discovered" it."

The second false premise was the doctrine of Manifest Destiny, buttressed by an unchristian interpretation of the biblical Exodus. In the 1840s the phrase "manifest destiny" came into use. The phrase was buried in a long essay in the July–August 1845 issue of *The United States Magazine, and Democratic Review* by the editor John L. O'Sullivan on the necessity of annexing Texas and the inevitability of American expansion. O'Sullivan was protesting European meddling in American affairs, especially by France and England, which he said were acting "for the avowed object of thwarting our policy and hampering our power, limiting our greatness and checking the fulfillment of our manifest destiny to overspread the continent allotted by Providence for the free development of our yearly multiplying millions." He expanded this idea on December 27, 1845, in a newspaper column in the *New York Morning News*. Discussing the dispute with Great Britain over the Oregon Country, O'Sullivan again cited the claim to "the right of our manifest destiny to overspread and to possess the whole of the continent which Providence has given us for the development of the great experiment of liberty and federated self-government entrusted to us."

Manifest Destiny expanded into the idea that the United States is destined by God to extend its dominion and spread democracy and capitalism across the entire North American continent. This philosophy drove nineteenth century U.S. territorial expansion and was used to justify the forced removal of Native Americans and other groups from their homes. The rapid expansion of the United States intensified the issue of slavery as new states were added to the Union, leading to the outbreak of the Civil War. Thanks to a high birth rate and brisk immigration, the U.S. population exploded in the first half of the nineteenth century, from around five million people in 1800 to more than twenty-three million by 1850. Such rapid growth—as well as two economic depressions in 1819 and 1839—would drive millions of Americans westward in search of new land and new opportunities.

President Thomas Jefferson kicked off the country's westward expansion in 1803 with the Louisiana Purchase, which at some 828,000 square miles nearly doubled the size of the United States and stretched from the Mississippi River to the Rocky Mountains. In addition to sponsoring the western expedition of Lewis and Clark of 1805–7, Jefferson also set his sights on Spanish Florida, a process that was finally concluded in 1819 under President James Monroe. But critics of that treaty faulted Monroe and his secretary of state, John Quincy Adams, for yielding to Spain what they considered legitimate claims on Texas, where many Americans continued to settle. In 1823, Monroe invoked Manifest Destiny when he spoke before Congress to warn European nations not to interfere with America's Westward expansion, threatening that any attempt by Europeans to colonize the "American continents" would be seen as an act of war. This policy of an American sphere of influence and of non-intervention in European affairs became known as the "Monroe Doctrine." After 1870, it would be used as a rationale for U.S. intervention in Latin America.

Another fruit of the Manifest Destiny ideology was the purchase of Alaska in 1867 which established US hegemony from the Atlantic to the Pacific oceans. The indigenous inhabitants were not granted automatic citizenship. Romantic nationalism, land hunger and the evangelical Second Great Awakening used this belief to justify the war with Mexico, the oppression of the Indian tribes, and expansion from the Atlantic Ocean to the Pacific Ocean.

As the boundaries of America grew, white settlers and proponents of expansion began to voice concerns over what they considered an obstacle to settlement and America's economic and social development—the American Indian tribes living on lands east of the Mississippi River which bordered white settlement. The land was home to many tribal nations

including the Cherokee, Creek and Seminole in the south and the Choc-
taw and Chickasaw in the west. That land held the promise of economic
prosperity to raise cattle, wheat, and cotton, and harvest timber and miner-
als. Eager to take possession of the land, the settlers began to pressure the
federal government to acquire the lands from the Indian tribes. To these
white settlers, the Indian tribes were standing in the way of progress and of
America's destiny

The concept of manifest destiny was used to rationalize the removal
of American Indians from their native homelands and enrich land speculators. In the minds of white Americans, the Indians were not using the
land to its full potential as they reserved large tracts of unspoiled land for
hunting, leaving the land uncultivated. If it was not being cultivated, then
the land was being wasted. Americans declared that it was their duty, their
manifest destiny, which compelled them to seize, settle, and cultivate the
land. Not surprisingly, the most active supporters of manifest destiny and
proponents of Indian removal were those who practiced land speculation.
Land speculators bought large tracts of land with the expectation that the
land would quickly increase in value as more people settled in the west and
demand for that western land increased. As the western land was admitted
into the Union, it would consequently increase in value.

The truth about the checkered history of how white settlers displaced
America's indigenous tribes has never been better told than by Dee Brown.[5]
It began when the Spanish explorer Christopher Columbus arrived at San
Salvador on October 12 1492. "So tractable, so peaceable are these people",
whom he called Indians, he wrote to Spain's King and Queen, "that I swear
in the world there is not a better nation. They love their neighbors as themselves, and their discourse is ever sweet and gentle, and accompanied with
a smile; and though it is true that they are naked, yet their manners are
decorous and praiseworthy". Yet as ever more settlers crashed in upon these
lands, ceremonies of mutual honor were brushed aside, the Indians were
marginalized, the best land was taken, opposition was quashed, massacres
took place. As even more settlers arrived, treaties were made and ignored,
whole tribes departed along their "trails of tears", and some were decimated
by western diseases. Native Americans believe that no treaty has been fully
kept by the US.

The truth about the pilgrim fathers whose coming is re-enacted at
every Thanksgiving needs to be put in its greater context. After the English

5. Brown, *Bury My Heart.*

28

refugees of conscience arrived at Plymouth in 1620 most of them would probably have starved to death had the natives not fed them. A group of them regarded the English as helpless children. They shared corn with them from the tribal stores, showed them how to catch fish, and helped them plant seeds once they had survived their first winter. They agreed a transfer of some land to these colonists. Soon, however, other colonists arrived in waves who swept aside such niceties and pushed the natives into the wilderness.

Wars took place. The "Cowboys and Indians" mythology filled western film screens, and the voice of the Creator in these precious children of the soil went unheeded. The US authorities took the line of divide and rule. They co-opted some Indians, made agreements with some tribal representatives, established reservations, but later revised these agreements as productive land became scarce. Attempts were made to assimilate Indians. Their children were sent to boarding schools where they spoke only English and had their hair cut short. Many were abused. Numerous Cherokee became successful "European" type plantation owners and business people. The Hopi people divided into two camps, the friendlies, who co-operated and the hostiles who did not.

Certain types of Bible believers justified Manifest Destiny in terms of their reading of the Bible. They were like Moses' people and America was their Promised Land. All three original colonies—James-town, Plymouth, and Massachusetts Bay—claimed in their founding charters that the land they secured already belonged to the English king regardless of whether it was occupied by Native tribes. Some of them likened the Natives to Canaanite tribes who were thought to be godless and should be marginalized or destroyed.[6]

They did not read the Old Testament in the light of the New Testament, and even their reading of the biblical accounts of Joshua were selective. They failed to read between the lines of the biblical accounts. Joshua had his construct of what was God's will. But God's captain said he was not on either side of these adversaries (Joshua 5:14). Joshua sought permission to pass through peaceably (Judges 11:12–28). The Promised land was a gift of God for establishing a place to live in His way (Chronicles 20:10–12) not a colonization for power. The original inhabitants had 400 years to discover how to live well, but they didn't make it. Israelites kept their promises: to the Gibeonites en route (Joshua 9:9–end); to Rahab in Jericho. They saved

---

6. Woodley, *Shalom*.

the fruit trees (Deuteronomy 20:19). They had a code of conduct toward women captives. When they had settled some peoples continued living in the land (Joshua 13:13), the Geshurites and Maacathites. They enacted laws to protect the alien. They integrated foreigners, e.g. Uriah the Hittite. An Ishmaelite was in charge of the king's camels (1 Chronicles 27:31). God remembered the covenant Israel made with the Gibeonites and held Israel accountable to it even though it was 400 years old (2 Samuel 21).

The Old Testament is the most honest of the world's scriptures. It admits that Israel became arrogant and turned to false gods, that it forfeited God's favor and was thus overruled and exiled; that it had got its image of its messiah wrong. The messiah would be a suffering servant and make a way for all nations to receive the light. Which of them applied Jesus's words in Luke 22:25–27 *"Jesus said to them, "The kings of the Gentiles lord it over them; and those who exercise authority over them call themselves Benefactors. But you are not to be like that. Instead, the greatest among you should be like the youngest, and the one who rules like the one who serves? For who is greater, the one who is at the table or the one who serves? Is it not the one who is at the table? But I am among you as one who serves""*

How many proponents of Manifest Destiny apply the following parable to themselves? *"There was a rich man . . . One day Lazarus, a diseased beggar, was laid at his gate longing for scraps from the rich man's table. The beggar died and was carried by the angels to be with Abraham in the place of the righteous dead. The rich man also died and his soul went into hell. There, in torment, he saw Lazarus in the far distance with Abraham. "Father Abraham," he shouted, "have some pity! Send Lazarus over here if only to dip the tip of his finger in water and cool my tongue, for I am in anguish in these flames." But Abraham said to him, "Son, remember that during your lifetime you had everything you wanted, and Lazarus had nothing. So now he is here being comforted and you are in anguish . . ." Then the rich man said, "O Father Abraham, then please send him to my father's home—for I have five brothers—to warn them about this place of torment lest they come here when they die." But Abraham said, "The Scriptures have warned them again and again. Your brothers can read them any time they want to." But Abraham said, "If they won't listen to Moses and the prophets, they won't listen even though someone rises from the dead.""* Selected from Luke 16:19–31 Living Bible (TLB).

Other Americans see their civilization more broadly as a fulfillment of the biblical mandate to humans to *"be fruitful and multiply, and fill the earth and subdue it, and have dominion over the fish of the sea and over the birds of the air and over every living thing that moves upon the earth*" (Genesis 1:28), but they apply this in an ethno-centric way. The American Heritage Dictionary of the English Language defines ethnocentrism as "the belief in the superiority of one's own cultural group". Cherokee Robert Francis has said: "Colonization begins with religion and specifically with a theology that serves to raise the colonizers above those to be colonized. Such theologies of conquest are most usually based on exclusive truth claims and exclusive notions of salvation . . . when a people develop the idea that they have exclusive possession of communication from God and exclusive control of the means of salvation, all peoples of earth stand in peril."[7] It was ethno-centrism that led to the crucifixion of Christ.

Randy Woodley concludes,

> "In this way the very foundation of . . . the American Dream was built on a mentality of theft, imperialism, and supposed superiority. They had no sense that the Native people were made in God's image and might have been put on the land by God. They seem not to have reflected upon Scripture verses such as *"Do you Israelites think you are more important to me than Ethiopians? I brought you out of Egypt, but have I not done as much for other nations too?"* (Amos 9:7)."[8]

This colonial re-writing of Scripture has led to what native American theologians describe as the heresy of White Supremacy, which is still ingrained in the White psyche. Dr. Martin Luther King Jr. became depressed in his last year. He concluded that even white Americans who demonstrated in favor of equal rights for black Americans did this as a charitable enterprise rather than because it was false science, and this disfigured the moral character of those who believed the lie. In his final book[9] he wrote "White America is not even psychologically organized to close the gap—essentially it seeks only to make it less painful and less obvious, but in most respects to retain it."

At the founding of the US, American citizenship was available exclusively to "free white persons." It took decades of struggle and a bloody civil war before citizenship was extended to formerly enslaved people and their descendants. Abraham Lincoln stated that he thought the Civil War was

7. Geeze Magazine Fall 2015 issue.

8. Woodley, *Shalom*

9. King Jr, *Where Do We Go*

God's judgement on America for slavery. In his second inaugural address, he suggested that "until all the wealth piled by the bondsman's two hundred and fifty years of unrequited toil shall be sunk, and until every drop of blood drawn with the lash shall be paid for by another drawn with the sword, as was said three thousand years ago, so still it must be said, "the judgements of the Lord are true and righteous altogether" ". Few realize that the US Capitol building was built by African slaves rented from their owners, or that many of America's Founding Fathers were slave owners who became rich off the land stolen from Native Americans. Greg Boyd cautions in his Christus Victor Ministries Blog "Until this destructive myth is dispelled . . . the American church will continue to look more like the racially divided, imperialistic, consumeristic, individualistic and hedonistic culture we live in than it will look like Jesus Christ."[10] Indigenous people, who were members of sovereign nations, did not have access to full citizenship until 1924. And for most of US history, race-based immigration laws, such as the Chinese Exclusion Act, prevented most immigrants from outside Western Europe from coming to US and claiming citizenship. Former Evangelicals such as Rob Bell, founder of a mega church in Grand Rapids, Michigan, who, following the publication of his book *Love Wins* in 2011 was ostracized by some of his followers, preaches that the Jesus movement was birthed as a counter to empire. He says "There is a religion more sacred to people than anything involving God, Jesus, the Bible—and that is America".[11] The twenty-first century fires and plagues that ravage America may be God's judgement upon her for slavery to money.

In 2017 Blackstone CEO Stephen A. Schwarzman published the ground-breaking book *What It Takes: Lessons in the Pursuit of Excellence*. He delineates the end of capitalism as we have known it. This is because, contrary to classical claims that in a free market economy money trickles down to the most needy, it is now possible for a tiny minority to keep most of the money. He is not against income inequality, but is against income insufficiency. He concludes that "we have stopped adequately preparing our population for the world that we're living in, let alone the world of the future in the information age". In a Time Magazine interview (December 2–9 2019) he concludes: "If you talk to the people running governments around the world, they'll tell you it's increasingly hard to run a liberal democracy. There's almost no issue today where very small groups of people

10. Boyd, *Lies My Teacher*
11. Bell, *Heresy, holiness, and Oprah*

aren't basically attacking the majority (through social media). And defeating what a majority wants to get their own way."

It is possible to promote the worship of God and to be in denial about unjust treatment of others through neglect. The prophet Nathan was an advisor to King David. He advised him against the empire-building tendency to build a huge temple in the name of God. He has God saying "I have not lived in a house since the day I brought up the people of Israel from Egypt to this day, but I have been moving about in a tent and a tabernacle. Wherever I have moved about among all the people of Israel, did I ever speak a word with any of the tribal leaders of Israel, whom I commanded to shepherd my people Israel, saying "Why have you not built me a house of cedar?" On another occasion he asked the king to adjudicate over a rich man who stole a poor man's sheep. David said the rich thief should be punished. Nathan said "You are the man", because David had "stolen" another man's wife and, as commander in chief, had arranged for her husband to be slain in battle. 2 Samuel 12. The mark of a true church is that it loves and listens to the people on its door-step.

The USA rightly threw off rule by a tyrannical English king, and in that cause declared that each man had the right to own a gun; but it missed out on the fact that every citizen is the son or daughter of a King, and that everyone, including women, blacks, and natives, bears God's royal likeness within them. Our truest freedom lies, not in becoming independent of all innate relationships and structures, but in bringing out the best in them all.

Christianity as a whole—though there have been some glorious exceptions—has to repent of its attachment to empire for much of its two thousand years. First it was Rome, then the Holy Roman Empire and then the trading empires that spread across the world from the seventeenth century. This has affected the Roman Catholic and Orthodox churches, and the state churches of England and Scandinavia. USA independent evangelical churches assume they are not tainted by this virus, but this is self-deception. They have colonized in the context of the market. This is what John Drane describes as the McDonaldization of the church. The supermarket mentality panders to essentially selfish ("what blesses me") desires. Worshippers criss-cross their cities to the ecclesiastical supermarket of their choice, sucking dry their neighborhoods.[12]

The freedom the New Testament promises us is to be free in Christ (Romans 6:22), who renounced his personal wishes in order to lay his life

---

12. Drane, *McDonaldization.*

down for humankind. George Monbiot's film *Capitalism is the Planet's Cancer* illustrates how capitalism seeks constant growth: it monetizes and marketizes nature and human communities. It has become like the Golden Calf that Aaron allowed the people to erect. This was in opposition to the Ten Commandments which God gave Moses as the basis for a civilized society.

Our lives are shaped by the narratives which dominate our culture. Dominant cultural narratives include consumerism, capitalism, individualism, that we can be whatever we want to be, that no one in public life can be trusted. Christian westerners too easily identify their land with Moses leading Israel to a promised land, while they fail to identify with the majority of Moses' people who worshipped a golden calf. Someone has paraphrased Romans 11:2 as follows: "Refuse to allow the dominant cultural narratives to have the last word in your heart and life. Immerse yourself in God's great story so that it captures your heart, fills your imagination and drives your life forward."

When citizens in certain US states whose governors had required them to stay at home in order to prevent a pandemic of the corona virus in 2020 packed the streets in protest, in the name of their God-given right to freedom, I tweeted: "Remind US protesters against lock-down that the freedom you give us is to walk humbly with you and to walk gently upon earth (Psalm 21), not to commit mass suicide." During the pandemic one pastor and his flock continued to crowd together for worship, saying that God would protect them. That pastor and a segment of his congregation died of the virus. The sands of their false faith narrative hit the rocks of reality—we are all connected and bound by biological and social laws.

The white American narrative is that it is based on freedom. God frees us to do, say, achieve anything lawful. Capitalism is the economic application of that principle. So when certain states required citizens to lock-down during the Covid-19 pandemic, there were street protests against this in the name of God, freedom, and America. As Americans more than any other people resisted social distancing in the name of freedom, so their deaths through Covid-19 rose higher than those of any other people.

I describe a cartoon during the Covid-19 pandemic. A USA state is in lock-down. Swimming pools are closed. But one defiant evangelical dives into the infected pool holding a placard "Freedom. Jesus". He does not see that the area all around is a plague-ridden wreck. He does not see that the creation beyond is poisoned and dying. He does not see Jesus weeping "If only you had recognized the things that make for your well-being" (Luke 19:41).

The truth needs to be told about broken promises. The newly formed American Congress promised on July 13th 1787 that the lands and property of the Indians "shall never be taken from them without their consent". No sooner was this promise made than it was broken. As large numbers of new settlers poured into the Ohio Valley bloody battles ensued and not one of the treaties was kept in its entirety. Over the following one hundred years at least one hundred and ninety documented treaties were ratified by the Congress: all were nullified in part because of the land-grabbing incomers. There are now over five hundred and sixty-two federally recognized tribes, but several hundred tribal groups still seek recognition and others have died out as a result of catching western diseases.

The truth needs to be told about the false gods of the settlers cloaked by religious piety. Indigenous people have always known many things that are wrong with White and Spanish Americans. The late Richard Twiss, a Sicangu Lakota, describes in his two compelling books[13, 14] how the "Christian" Cowboys made land possession and money their gods. We cannot repent, however, if we don't understand the nature or feel the cost of our sins.

The truth needs to be told about the obliteration of wholesome elements of native spirituality. The last of the great Sioux chiefs died in the battle at Wounded Knee, Pine Ridge at Christmas 1890. Black Elk surveyed the scene and said: "A people's dream died there. There is no center any longer, and the sacred tree is dead."

The sacred tree, however, is universal. After a century during which white America's economy and to a great extent its religion became a prisoner of consumerism and self-made false images, even some settlers could no longer be deaf to the Creator's whisper rising from the trampled earth.

Separation

The second twin tower is Separation. Non-Native westerners, including Christians, are split people. They have ceased to be holistic. Separation splits what the Creator intends to be part of a greater whole into disconnected individual units.

---

13. Twiss, *Rescuing the Gospel*
14. Twiss, *One Church*

The biblical teaching of shalom is derived from a root denoting wholeness. It means harmony between myself, my neighbor, my family, my own and neighboring peoples, and the earth. It is a cosmic principle. It is a way of being. The kingdom of God, in contrast to the kingdoms of human elites, is relational. It is about everyone reaching their potential in community. The significance of shalom includes the political domain—the absence of war and enmity; and the social—the absence of strife, and the right ordering of relationships, and meeting of needs.

However, the Gospel of Jesus Christ spread into the Greek-speaking world. The Greek understanding of the world was dualistic. Plato thought that soul is immortal and the body is just a temporary reflection, so it is not that important. In dualism spirit is split from matter, mind from the body, commerce from morality, earth from heaven.

The Western Church moved from Hebrew holism to Greek dualism. Augustine is known as the Father of the Western Church by both Catholic and Reformed Christians. He supplies us with a treasury of insights. However, he was a dualist and a Neo-Platonist. As a former Manichee he despised the material. Augustine had big insights, but because of the anti-material bias of his Neoplatonism (i.e. matter is evil), Augustine turned away from God's self-revelation throughout time and throughout the cosmos. Sin separated humans and creation from God. So, he thought, we became trash. Augustine presented the Savior as separated from the Trinity and coming from outside of creation and humanity to save selected individuals. Jesus had to come down from the blue yonder, like a Spiderman, to rescue individual souls and whisk them off to a heaven that was separated from this world, when all the time the Trinity is within all.

Europe's sixteenth century church reformers inherited this fault-line. A major seam of Western theologies of both Roman and Reformed churches contains seeds of this heresy of separation—separation of the spiritual from the material, of the saved from the damned, of the present from the future, of private faith from the world of work and government, of the individual from the wider community, of Christ from the earth.

The Reformation indirectly influenced the seventeenth to eighteenth century rationalist movement known as the Enlightenment which extended these ideas. The Rationalist Enlightenment separated thought from the rest of human existence, hence Descartes' famous saying "Cogito, ergo sum" (I think therefore I am). Soon you could separate much of life into compartments: faith is separate from public life, morals are separate from business.

Because of the lack of holistic theology Christianity retreated into splits, private bible reading and private Sunday worship in D.I.Y. churches. This truncated Christianity became the enemy of science, of human values, of the common good. It is why some of the Reformed traditions have treated the earth as an inert object to be plundered at will by humans. Scientific developments such as the theory of evolution coincided with a prevalent non-holistic theology that pictured God as a clock-maker up above watching his clock—the universe—tick away. No wonder so many Americans think science is not compatible with faith.

The American historian Lynn White claimed that Christianity "has made it possible to exploit nature in a mood of indifference to the feelings of natural objects . . . We shall continue to have a worsening ecologic crisis until we reject the Christian axiom that nature has no reason for existence save to serve man."[15, 16]

US culture allows that human rights are God-given, but these concern only the individual in isolation. It fails to guard God's inalienable relationship with the human family and all creation. It fails to recognize that we exist in relationship. Our validation as humans rests not in rights over against others, but as members of a human family sustained by God's love. "Not wounding one's neighbor—that is the way of Christ" said the 6th century Palestinian monk Barsanuphius. To isolate the individual from the communion inherent in God in humankind, is a deadly oversight such as that which banished humans from the Garden of Eden. To allow the economy to assume a life of its own free from the moral norms God has implanted in human consciousness is also to make money our god.

The "might is right" principle is disguised and dispersed, but in 1999 the USA Energy Secretary Bill Richardson made this rare admission: "Oil has literally made [USA] foreign and security policy for decades . . . it has provoked the division of the Middle East . . . the Arab Oil Embargo; Iran versus Iraq; the Gulf War. This is all clear."

This foreign policy is irrelevant to individual worshippers. So many American evangelicals interpret righteousness as personal piety when it actually means acting rightly towards one's community. Millions who are taught to accept Jesus as their personal Savior are like those religious zealots in the Gospels who rejected Jesus because he refused to be the Messiah they had made in their own image. The Messiah who wept over Jerusalem

15. White, Jr *Historical Roots*
16. Middelmann, *Pollution*

wept over their failure to embrace community. Those who had only personal piety would not understand how creation could shudder when the Son of God was crucified—the earth quaked and the sun hid its light. Native peoples often understand more about what makes for good human and earth community than do individualistic Christians who dismiss anything that makes for community as an aberration of "liberals".

The Civil War illustrates the heresy of Separation. American white settlers threw off British colonial rule in 1776, but continued to colonize "their" new land on the back of slave labor. In the British Empire William Wilberforce's long Parliamentary campaign succeeded in abolishing the slave trade in the British Empire in 1833, but America's now independent colonies continued it. In the state of Columbia many of Washington's iconic buildings, including the Whitehouse, were built by black slave labor in the ensuing years. The American Civil War of 1861–1865 was about the rights of states to maintain plantations of black slaves without votes or citizens' rights. The southern states were pro-slavery. Even after slavery was made illegal in 1865 systemic racism remained deeply rooted, as the Civil Rights movement led by Dr. Martin Luther King Jr. in the 1960s and the Black Lives Matter movement of our time reveal. It remains deeply rooted in police forces, appointments systems, educational curricula, and in the white "Christian" psyche.[17]

More generally, separation has been built into the psyche and also the organization of western Christianity. Let us be absolutely clear: the present divisions between sections/denominations of the Christian Church are a violation of the New Testament model of the church. So often we hear schism justified by leaders who say theirs is the true church. But referring to the universal church the apostle Paul writes in 1 Corinthians 12: "*For just as the body is one and has many members . . . so it is with Christ . . . But God has so arranged the body . . . that there be no dissension within the body*" 1 Corinthians 12:12, 24, 25. He is here referring to the universal Body of Christ. Christians as individuals are only morons said James Houston of Regents College, Vancouver. The Apostles Creed refers to the "one, holy, catholic and apostolic church".

David Cole points out[18] that current western political systems undermine the biblical understanding of the Trinity as relationship. The Enlightenment philosophers such as Thomas Hobbes and John Locke thought that

17. The New York Times Podcast 1619
18. The Aidan Way Issue 98

38

the goal of human life was to attain one's own independence. They argued that relationships tend to weaken one's independence and thus undermine one's humanity. Such reasoning subtly sidelines God or gives rise to an understanding of God who is but a sovereign, independent individual. As a result capitalism and liberalism became the goal of politics.

The marks of the church's catholicity are baptism, Holy Communion and the service of the weaker churches by the stronger in a world-wide communion of love. *"If one part of the body suffers, all the other parts share its suffering . . . As in the natural body of a human, the members should be closely united by the strongest bonds of love"* 1 Corinthians 12:26. Christians who operate without yielding to God within the other members of Christ's Body would be like the Father, Christ or the Spirit operating without yielding to the other: unthinkable.

Pope Francis sees this. He has tried to represent centuries of split Catholic teaching on the environment in his Encyclical *Laudato Si,* and in opening up the Vatican's Ethnological Museum's Soul of the World (Anima Mundi). At its opening the Pope said: "I think that the Vatican Museums are called increasingly to become a living "home", inhabited by and open to all, with the doors wide open to populations from all over the world. A place where all may feel represented; where it can be perceived in a tangible way that the gaze of the Church precludes no-one . . . Those who enter here should feel that there is room in this house for them too, for their people, their tradition, their culture: the European and the Indian, the Chinese and the native of the Amazonian or Congolese forest, of Alaska or of the Australian deserts or of the islands of the Pacific. All peoples are here, in the shadow of the dome of Saint Peter's, close to the heart of the Church and to the Pope. And this is because art is not something rootless: art is born of the heart of peoples. It is a message: from the heart of one people to another. Beauty unites us. It invites us to experience human fraternity, contrasting the culture of resentment, racism, nationalism, which is always lurking."

Many Conservative Evangelicals who formed a base for President Trump have yet to catch up. My friend Baxter Kruger, an evangelical theologian and pastor, has authored several books that seek to remedy this heresy of separation for western readers and to restore our understanding of the Trinity as an eternal Communion.[19, 20]

19. Kruger, *Jesus*
20. Kruger, *Great Dance*

For Christians in Eastern and Celtic lands the Trinity does not stay separated. The Trinity is not a sub-division of the doctrine of God, the Trinity is the heart of all reality. The Father, Jesus and the Spirit are not only the beginning and end of everything in the cosmos, they are inside the cosmic process, inside humans. All things subsist in the Word (John 1:4). Greg Goebel, a priest of the Anglican Church in North America, said this in a sermon about the Trinity as a model: "In our human world, we are always caught between union and personality. If a couple or a group of people decide to unite, we always end up squashing the individual personalities of the couple or group in some way. So we react to that, and we declare independence, we celebrate the individual. And then in doing so, we swing to the other side and we damage community. We don't have a full experience of full union and community that does not in any way destroy personality and individual existence."

The New Testament scholar N.T. Wright exposes the falsity of this splitting theology in the book *The Day the Revolution Began*[21] He writes about old ideas based on the Augustinian split:

> ". . . the awful thing is that this message about an angry God and an innocent victim has a lot more in common with ancient Pagan thought than with ancient Jewish or Christian thought . . . the last great scene in the Bible is not about saved souls going up to heaven as most of the medieval mystery plays would have it, but about the new Jerusalem coming down from heaven to earth so that heaven and earth are joined together."

"Ideas create idols; only wonder leads to knowing" wrote Gregory of Nyssa. The history of Protestantism has been described as the history of opinions. Each person has their own opinion! Eugene Peterson wrote[22] "We have become consumers of packaged spiritualities. This is idolatry . . . The Christian market in idols has never been more brisk or lucrative". Redemption cannot come to the West until it sees with its own eyes how much of its "Christian" razzmatazz has a spirit of fragmentation. *You may be part of a cult . . . if you show higher respect for the American flag than the cross; if you think God loves America first, and everybody else second; if you worship a refugee on Sunday and ignore one on Monday.* Shane Claiborne tweet.

Because churches have been separated from the Christ who is The Ground of Being (Tillich) they have become fragmented and many have

21. Wright, *Day the Revolution Began*.
22. Peterson, *Christ*.

become nationalistic. It happened in England at the time of the Reformation. Many Orthodox churches have fallen into this trap; it is happening in Russia today. And it is happening in USA. To challenge an action or a word of the President becomes the unforgivable sin. Gone is the modern equivalent of Nathan the prophet who confronted his king, David, with the words "Your behavior is like that of a hungry traveler": when he asked for food from a rich farmer with many sheep the farmer killed a poor neighbor's only sheep for him to eat (2 Samuel 12). Many evangelical churches write off liberal churches as unbiblical without realizing that they themselves are unbiblical. The bedrock of the Judaeo-Christian heritage is the Ten Commandments. The bedrock of the Ten Commandments is *"You shall have no gods but me"* Exodus 20:2 and Deuteronomy 5:6. Yet ever after nations and churches have promoted the false god of "my nation first" in the name of God. Moses worshipped the god of his tribal forebears. That was all he knew. That was his construct. The construct was not evil, but it was inadequate. He had to learn to outgrow it. Exodus 3:13–15. He asked his god what Divine name he should use when he talked to the Emperor (Pharaoh) of Egypt. He was told to use the phrase "I am what I am" (Yahweh). Buddhists might use the term Being. That is, we cannot manipulate God, or cast God in our own image, or in our national image. God is Reality. Yet we identify God with our national flag. We invoke God's name in support of our wars.

The "church" of Jesus's day (the Jewish temple and synagogues) was often run by Pharisees. The word Pharisee meant a separatist. They kept separate from gentiles and from anything unclean. In contrast, Jesus made contact with the outsiders, the marginalized and the unclean. Jesus told some Pharisees that they were putting on a false show, they were not authentic. The Pharisee tendency is not just among Jews, it continues also in churches. It is easy to make God in our own image by projecting on to the Bible our limited, prejudiced mindsets. Some Pharisees who met Jesus were devoted Bible students but they fell into this trap. They made God's Word ineffective because they promoted their own selfish opinions as if they were what the Bible taught, Mark 7:12. Followers of Jesus are not meant to enslave themselves to the letter of its laws, but rather to understand and live by the spirit of its teachings.

Jesus mentions the church only twice in the Gospels, but he mentions the Kingdom over a hundred times. The kingdom embraces heaven and earth and social justice. The church is an expression of the kingdom—and a vehicle for it. We have to guard against the Pharisee Tendency creeping into the church that is more concerned about ritual and religion than about the well-being of humans and the earth.

The Falling Sky: Words of a Yanomami Shaman[23] tells how deforestation in the Amazon foretells the end of the world: "The earth's skin is beautiful and sweet smelling. The white people only know how to abuse and spoil the forest. They destroy everything in it, the earth, the trees, the hills, the rivers until they have made its ground bare and blazing hot. All that remains is a soil that has lost its breath of life."

> The whites, too, shall pass—perhaps sooner than other tribes. Continue to contaminate your own bed, and you will one night suffocate in your own waste. Chief Seattle.

But repentance is possible.

In June 2018 Dave Bookless, Director of A Rocha, was profoundly challenged by Australia Aboriginal speakers at an Oceana conference on Creation Care and the Gospel, part of the Lausanne World Evangelical Alliance Creation Care Network. One Aboriginal speaker, Brooke Prentis, presented a powerful paper she'd jointly written with a non-Aboriginal theologian about "Learning to be Guests of Ancient Hosts on Ancient Lands". It included uncomfortable reminders of the arrogance of many European Christians who saw Aboriginal peoples as "ignorant pagans", ignoring that it was God who placed Aboriginal peoples in the land and taught them how to care for it for so many millennia. Brooke reminded us that much of the wisdom Aboriginal Christians have imbibed from their ancestors is deeply biblical yet has been lost in Western Christianity: the land as "hosting all living creatures with its riches, providing and sustaining life. The land holds the people, and the people hold the land. We as aboriginal peoples . . . have been given the responsibility from Creator Spirit to care for the land . . . and to nurture the land." As somebody who heard from childhood that "this earth is not my home" and has had to rediscover the biblical wisdom that we cannot relate to God outside the places and communities God plants us in, I was deeply moved by this and by the grace, welcome and forgiveness shown by the Aboriginal Christians at the conference. However, the most disturbing and moving words came from another indigenous Christian leader, this time from the island nation of Tuvalu.

23. Kopenawa with Albert, *Falling Sky*

Rev Aso Loapo is a Congregationalist Minister who also works for Tuvalu Climate Action Network (TUCAN). He explained that in Tuvalu and many other Pacific island nations, Land + Oceans + People + God = life. When this four-fold unity is broken, death follows. Today with Climate Change causing sea-level rise, dangerous storms, and coral bleaching, Tuvalu is threatened with complete submersion and people are asking, "Where are you, God?" Having heard of the covenant God made with Noah and all creation never again to destroy the earth by water, they ask "Why doesn't God see that we are sinking? Does God punish the innocent for the sins of the rich?" The cry of the people of Tuvalu is a cry of those who belong to the land and oceans and who say, "We cannot simply get up and move. We have strong links to our motherland." As Christians—particularly those of us in the world's richer nations—we need to hear these painful questions from our sisters and brothers, which I believe are addressed more to us than to God. We need to lament and repent for our cultural and spiritual blindness, and our greedy wasteful lifestyles. We need to pray for and listen with humility to those who have stewarded God's world far better than us. Every church should seek to green the earth.

In his Exhortation[24] Pope Francis writes, "To sustain a lifestyle which excludes others, or to sustain enthusiasm for that selfish ideal, a globalization of indifference has developed. Almost without being aware of it, we end up being incapable of feeling compassion at the outcry of the poor, weeping for other people's pain, and feeling a need to help them, as though all this were someone else's responsibility and not our own. The culture of prosperity deadens us; we are thrilled if the market offers us something new to purchase. In the meantime, all those lives stunted for lack of opportunity seem a mere spectacle; they fail to move us." He defines meekness as a counter-cultural virtue that saves us from being exhausted by constantly trying to dominate and control.

Peter Scazzero[25] helps church leaders face up to the fact that we all have what Jung termed our Shadow. The Shadow consists of the unacceptable parts of ourselves that we have repressed, and which we project on to others. Every church and every country has a Shadow. Before Jesus could begin his public ministry, he had to face up to his Shadow during forty days of testing in the wilderness. Many churches find their well-being through great buildings/organisation, great programmes and great promotion. They

24. Pope Francis, *Gaudete et Exultate*
25. Scazzero, *Emotionally Healthy*

43

do this in the name of Christ. Scazzero points out that church leaders who do not face up to these three dark places in their Shadow are unhealthy, and so are their churches.

The three things Jesus faced in his forty days of testing in the wilderness were: To find his identity in what he had, in what he did, and what other people thought of him. He emerged finding his identity in knowing and doing his Father's will. He did not need to have anything, achieve anything, prove anything. Jesus temptations in the desert would have taken him down a false path of wrong identity. We all face the temptation to find our identity in 1) what we do (performance) 2) what we have (power and possession); 3) what others think of us (popularity). Performance, power, possessions and popularity. Peter Scazzero who is a great proponent of natural godly rhythms says "true freedom comes when we no longer need to be someone special in the eyes of others because we know we are loveable and good enough."

Jesus did not submit to these pressures in part because he had already been affirmed in his identity when at his baptism his Father said "You are my beloved Son". He was rooted deeply in his own true self and the calling upon his life. That inner vision motivated him to shun the false expectations of his family, his closest friends, and the religious community. He could say of Satan, the god of this world "he has nothing in me." It led him to the Cross. This inner reality freed him to preach and pursue the kingdom of God. Is the root of our twin tower evils that we are insecure as to our identity as persons and churches? The True Self as it is in Christ does not cling; it is free to sing, to laugh, to cry, to run or to dance. The True Self does not blame; it is free to embrace or bless, to play or pray for mercy. The True Self does not hide; it is free to celebrate or share, to communicate, to glow. The True Self does not boast; it enjoys its own being, its pulses and pastimes and those of others. The True Self does not possess; it receives all as a gift, and gives itself to others without conditions. In this understanding, churches are no longer centers whose entrance qualification is a list of beliefs or practices—they are centers where we share with all people a journey of becoming real. We no longer impose our own culture, our own pre-suppositions and Bible constructs on others—we become authentic. And we no longer judge others.

The Risen Christ inspired John the Beloved to write letters to seven churches in the region that is now Turkey (Revelation 1–3). He commended certain actions or qualities of some churches, but in each church, he identified something that was wrong for which he called them to repent. The Risen Christ desires to communicate with each local church in USA. What might commend their industry and other things. What might he expose, and call them to repent of? "You have glued your worship of me to the false god that you harbor. This false god I call "America First: right or wrong". You have separated yourselves from I AM—the God of all people. Let go of your false attachments. Put me first." To another church I sense he writes "You have tried to tear me from my Universal Body. Learn to know and love me in my weakest members—Palestinian believers walled off from their families and farmsteads, persecuted believers in Pakistan, believers who vote for the opposite political party to you, demeaned First Nation peoples on your doorstep . . . please me by demonstrating that in my Body the strong cherish the weak and learn from them . . ."

The Creator's Imprints in Modern America

A saying that relates to pre-Christian peoples to whom missionaries bring the Gospel has become common coinage: Christ confirms what is good in the culture, corrects what is bad, and reveals fresh expressions of love. It is right that we apply this truth to nominal and post-Christian cultures as well as to indigenous cultures. It would be wrong to dismiss everything to do with the west as empire building and fragmentation, and its churches as fake. We need to look with unjaundiced eyes for the Creator's imprints in western society, too. What are these?

The historian Tom Holland has written a series of books on the world's great civilisations. His latest book,[26] mercilessly exposes faults of the church—the massacres of non-Christians, the burning of heretics, the use of force in evangelizing America). His researches have led him to become a believer. He is convinced that the dignity of human life and equal rights of all races and genders flows from the Christian teaching that all humans are made in God's image (Genesis 1:26) and that the Divinity, becoming incarnate in human flesh, makes all peoples "one in Christ Jesus" (Galatians 3:28).Christianity injected into the Roman empire the insight that all human beings had intrinsic value as reflectors of God, regardless of any particular role. It was widely perceived that churches were mini welfare states, tending to treat the most needy.

26. Holland *Dominion*

The apostle Paul's revolutionary statement that all races, classes and genders are "one in Christ" (Galatians 3:28) lit a slow fuse that over the centuries exploded into social transformation.

Almost all pre-Christian peoples were patriarchal, and treated women as the property of men—they had no conjugal rights. The sixth century Frankish King Chilperic gave women equal rights with men because "my children came equally from God". The Christian Church came to believe that in a marriage both the man and the woman were joined as Christ was joined to his bride, the church. Sex was sacred and was an expression of holy communion. Marriage became a sacrament.

The doctrine that all people are created in God's image (Genesis 1:26) was modeled for all when God took human form in Christ. As a Christian understanding took root people realized that human rights needed to be enshrined in law. Gratian determined that the law should no longer exist to uphold the differences in status that chiefs and kings had taken for granted, its purpose was to uphold the rights of every individual for each was equally a child of God. In 1140 this was written into his *Decretals,* which became the text book for the Roman Church's canon law.

England's King Alfred, inspired by the Bible, collected law codes and by the time of Queen Elizabeth 1, rich and poor alike had the right to take an injustice to a judge. England's Magna Carta ensured that no individual had absolute power: it brought in some checks and balances to Government. Principles of the Magna Carta were enshrined in the USA Constitution. The Separation of powers was a recognition that "power corrupts and absolute power corrupts absolutely" (Acton). So modern America's Founding Fathers built in checks and balances and shared power between three independent branches of Government: The Legislative, composed of the House and Senate; The Executive, composed of the President, Vice-President, and the Departments; The Judiciary, composed of the federal courts and the Supreme Court. Each of these powers is limited, or checked, by another branch. Separation of Powers does not prevent empire building when a group mind-set takes over, but it does prevent excesses of empire building by a dictator. Similarly, the separation of church from state enables religions to have a voice but not a vote. Are not these imprints of the Creator?

Abolition of slavery and child labor and the rights of all adults to vote came later. Slavery—of blacks, browns, and whites—was found in most of the large civilisations: Babylonian, Egyptian, Persian, Chinese, Roman,

Islamic, and in African countries, before it came to European and American civilization. It was ended in the British Empire and later in America as a result of a Christian bad conscience. Those who opposed slavery won the civil war. Slavery was abolished in 1865. USA women got the right to vote in 1920. African Americans got the right to vote in 1965.

Although the narrative of America's Day of Thanksgiving, which Abraham Lincoln instituted in 1863, almost wrote out of the script the rape of America's indigenous peoples and the Puritan separatists were re-branded as "Pilgrims", in recent years attempts have been made to align Thanksgiving celebrations with reality. The Thanksgiving Play by Larissa Fast-Horse, a member of the Rosebud Sioux Tribe in the Sicanga Lakota Nation, has become one of the most produced plays in the U.S. Visitors to the National Museum of the American Indian who hope to learn a better way to teach the Thanksgiving story may learn that early Thanksgivings celebrated the burning of a Pequot village in 1637 and the killing of Wampanong leader Massasoit's son. So, the devout, well-meaning Pilgrim Fathers, who became an archetype of the White American psyche, carried a fundamental flaw. Now their blindness and spiritual arrogance is named and shamed, while continuing to thank God for the good elements in their coming.

Countless Americans who are against the state subsidizing the poor have, out of love of Christ's example, given generously of their money or time to serve those in greater need than themselves. The philanthropist Andrew Carnegie famously said that a kept dollar is a stinking dollar. More Americans serve overseas as missionaries than do those from any other country.

Millions of poor people from all continents embrace "the American dream" that anyone can start with nothing and rise to the top with hard work, ability and maybe some luck This "rags to riches" agenda need not, in principle, require mistreatment of others, though it often does. This dream is, however, becoming deja vue. Immigration controls have increased, as has the proportion of top people who have inherited their wealth.

The love of exploring, the study of science, the genius of inventing, the power of organizing and the creation of civil society—a space between the government and the individual where groups and institutions can operate without requiring permission—are perhaps other imprints of the Creator. I have noticed that Indians who have been traumatized by their mistreatment over generations seem happy to have smart phones, computers, cars, roads, mains water supplies, supermarkets, and state schools. Could these good things also be part of the Creator's imprints?

Another imprint of the Creator are the few glorious exceptions to Whites mistreating the First Nation peoples. The Quaker William Penn kept a 70-year covenant with the Indians of Pennsylvania, although he had black slaves, unlike his fellow Quaker Benjamin Lay who campaigned ceaselessly for the end of black slavery. Just as the godly colony of New England had been founded as a model for the world, so was "the city of love", Philadelphia, a huge area granted to Penn by royal charter. It became a haven of tolerance. It was New England that largely provided the founders of USA with a model of democracy and Pennsylvania with its model of tolerance. "The foundation of our Empire was not laid in the gloomy age of Ignorance and Superstition", declared George Washington, "but at an Epoch when the rights of mankind were better understood and more clearly defined than at any former period."[27] Although they were often blind to the implications of their enlightenment for Native Americans, they believed that they were the first fruits of a new era where there is neither Jew nor Gentile but all are one in Christ Jesus' (Galatians 3:28).

Others also stood with the tribes against their oppressors. The colonizing Spanish Empire of the fifteenth and sixteenth centuries was the most powerful kingdom in Christendom. It used military force to extend its boundaries. Even in the Americas its Franciscans came with the Bible in one hand and the sword in the other to enforce the conversion of indigenous peoples. When Christian scholars sought to justify this they turned to Aristotle rather than to the Church Fathers. However, many Dominicans, informed more by the tradition of Alcuin, who persuaded the Holy Roman Emperor Charlemagne to eschew violence and embrace love as a means of conversion, challenged the right of fellow settlers to keep the Indians in servitude. One colonist had a conversion like that of the apostle Paul on the road to Damascus. Bartholomew of Casas freed his slaves, and devoted himself to defending the Indians from tyranny: "they are our brothers, and Christ gave his life for them". He objected to Spanish imperialism in royal courts and simple settlements, he affirmed "Jesus Christ, the king of kings, was sent to win the world, not with armies, but with holy preachers, as sheep among wolves."[28]

---

27. Vile, *Constitutional Convention of 1787.*

28. Holland, *Dominion* .292.

Elements of USA democracy are perhaps another imprint of the Creator. Winston Churchill said that democracy is the worst form of Government except for all the others. Despite its empire-building and blindness, some imprints of the Creator might be discerned even by those who have been most hurt by the USA system. "All men are created equal" said the American constitution. When the founders spoke of "we, the people", it is true they were not talking about black people, women or Native Americans. However, although these were at first overlooked, the ideal is right. Joseph J. Ellis, the best-selling author on what the Founders got wrong, was asked what would unite all Americans. He replied "A great crisis that leaves us no choice but to come together. When the coastal areas have to be evacuated, when the real implications of climate change begin to hit, we're going to be forced to come together". (Time Magazine October 29 2018.) The USA and western Europe established other freedoms such as freedom of the press, which is now under threat through social media brainwashing. "Freedom of the press ensures that the abuse of every other freedom can be known, can be challenged and even defeated" said Kofi Annan, former UN General Secretary (died 2018).

During my last visit to USA I realized that USA is more deeply polarized than ever before. Those on the Right (Republicans) had rage and were broken hearted by the Left: those on the Left had rage and were broken hearted by the Right. For those on the Right America stands for the "can do" approach. Each person is responsible to work hard, use their talents, rise as high as they can. The state should have a smaller role (defense and security) and should not hand out subsidies that create dependency. Many Republicans are evangelical Christians: they condemn abortion as mass murder and put their energies into saving lost souls—they don't waste time with saving this earth or making sure that those infants they have saved are fed and clothed. For those on the Left America had "lost all moral compass", it did not care about the poor, the migrants, justice or the environment—the things Jesus called us to care about. Community, and the community of nations, were being destroyed. Is the imprint of the Creator seen in those few Christians who say "It is neither Right nor Left, but Straight—each person has a God-given responsibility; the State also has certain responsibilities. It is not one against the other, it is both for the Higher Good".

Respect is another imprint of the Creator. From the Christian Gospel we inherit virtues such as belief in the innate dignity of every human being, putting the interests of others above our own, and doing what's right. The life of Jesus Christ shows up the vacuity of utilitarianism, and inspires sacrifice for a higher cause. The truth that all people inherit the dignity of being made in the Creator's image may have been selectively applied, but its seeds may yet come to full flower. Black voices of integrity point out that not all white people are innately prejudiced—if they were, what room would there be for repentance? And not all white people have privilege. Some black people have better jobs, housing, and privileges than some white people. Larry Elder, a black radio commentator argues that the absence of black fathers is more responsible for behavior problems in young blacks than is a predominantly white police force.

Is caring capitalism another imprint of the Creator? Adam Smith's great work *The Wealth of Nations*[29] is still thought to provide a primary rationale for capitalism. He argued that free trade, private enterprise, and government that limits itself to basic services such as defense, justice, education, and transport lead to the best kind of society. The profit motive can be self-fulfilling as much as selfish; it brings wealth that is passed on to both rich and poor. This optimism was based on two underlying assumptions that have almost evaporated from our world. The first assumption was Smith's belief that people more or less adhered to a universal moral law. In *The Theory of Moral Sentiments*[30] he referred to "an invisible hand" by which wealth is passed from the rich to the poor through consumption and investment: "All the members of human society stand in need of each other's assistance . . . where the necessary assistance is reciprocally afforded . . . the society flourishes and is happy." His second assumption was that the entrepreneur made money while working through the family and the company as local, social and responsible units. The Industrial Revolution, however, divorced work from these responsible, mutually caring institutions. The decisions of multinational companies, some of them near monopolies, are divorced from the human and moral feelings of the vast numbers who supply, work for or buy products from them. It seems probable that Adam Smith would have sought to put right these degrading developments and that he would have demanded that monolithic power structures and price rings are held accountable.

Although from an indigenous perspective White America has grown rich by stealing their land and downgrading their dignity, from a White American point of view America is based upon the concept of freedom.

29. Smith, *Wealth of Nations*.
30. Smith, *Theory of Moral Sentiments*

There is freedom to vote, travel, speak, and work. Freedom also carries the idea that God gives us freedom to use our time and talents to improve ourselves, to create wealth, to achieve, to get to the top. It feeds the "rags to riches" American dream. Freedom has been mis-used, but the idea that each person is created free by God to fulfill their unique calling on earth is of abiding worth.

Is another imprint of the Creator the re-thinking that white Americans are embracing re racism and sexism? As many white as black Americans demonstrate for Black Lives Matter. The cowboy has long been a potent symbol of white American identity: rugged frontier warriors who embodied the quest for individual achievement, and for manifest destiny. In fact, one in four cowboys was black. A new generation of black artists has fashioned what is known as the Yeehaw Agenda. In fashion, film, and pop music this contests the very idea of American identity.

Angry Americans who wish "a plague upon you all" need to see the Creator's imprints in non-native Americans of all colors, including Christians. Some dismiss everything about Christendom and the historic top-down churches. But wherever any leader or member has sincerely sought to carry out "the Father's will", there Jesus has been. We too easily forget that Christianity at first spread among slaves, that countless renewals started with work among the poor, that bad people have been made better, and that many saintly people can inspire us to live closer to our Maker. In my own country of Britain, the King of England made himself the (human) head of The Church of England and threatened to imprison dissenters who later became Pilgrim Fathers of America. Yet many social reforms were brought about by members of that church: humane prisons (Elisabeth Fry), decent hospital care (Florence Nightingale) the end of Child Labor (Anthony Ashley-Cooper). We need to notice the good plants that have grown among the weeds.

There is no point in promoting "white guilt", nor in airbrushing out native failings: there is every point in listening to this "whisper from the trampled earth" and in evoking true godliness.

A Dark Age or a Golden Age?

Despite the fact that certain imprints of the Creator may be discerned in western culture, much is sick at its heart. Edward Gibbon's classic study *The Rise and Fall of the Roman Empire* has led countless others to analyse the elements that lead to the rise and fall of civilisations. Many contemporary commentators believe that the dominance of western lands has reached its peak, and decline has begun.

A further factor which causes thoughtful Americans to question their society is the mushrooming of false media. Richard Stengel[31] reveals that by 2015 experts realized that much Russian disinformation came from an anonymous building in St. Petersburg run by a shadowy company named The Internet Research Agency (IRA). Hundreds of young people daily send tweets and other social media under multiple accounts trashing democratic forces in USA and in Europe. This may be just the thin end of the wedge. A post-truth culture calls for all Christians to stand for truth wherever it may lead.

The time has come to re-appraise "Christian America" for several more reasons. Lamin Sanneh's volume in *Oxford Studies in World Christianity*[32] reveals an astonishing shift in the world focus of Christianity. He concludes that Christianity "is now in the twilight of its Western phase and is at the beginning of its formative non-Western impact". In 1950 some 80 per cent of the world's Christians lived in the northern hemisphere in Europe and America. By 2005 the vast majority of Christians lived in the southern hemisphere in Asia, Africa, and Latin America. It is a continental shift of historic proportions. This shift rides on the back of an inter-cultural approach to conversion.

Today, voices of young climate change protesters from white nations also question the western narrative. "How dare you?" sixteen-year-old Greta Thunberg challenged the 2019 UN General Assembly in New York, in the presence of Donald Trump. "We are in the beginning of a mass extinction and all you can talk about is money and fairy tales of eternal economic growth".

> "The White man does not understand America. He is too far removed from its formative processes. The roots of the tree of his life have not yet grasped the rock and the soil . . . Men must be born and reborn to belong. Their bodies must be formed of the dust of their forefathers' bones." Chief Luther Standing Bear, Lakota.

Otto Scharmer, Senior Lecturer, MIT. Co-founder, Presencing Institute. www.ottoscharmer.com argues that we are dealing with a profound

31. Stengel, *Information Wars*
32. Sanneh, *Disciples of All Nations*

axial shift, a new polarity that is redefining the coordinates of the political, economic, and cultural space. He contrasts the Closed and Open mind-sets. "Closed" means a mindset that amplifies the triad of Fear, Hate, and Ignorance. It's a mindset that manifests in the form of five behaviors: blinding (not seeing reality); de-sensing (not empathizing with others); absencing (losing the connection to one's highest future); blaming others (an inability to reflect); and destroying (destruction of nature, of relation-ships, and of self). These behaviors are now weaponized with social media mechanisms such as micro-targeting and dark posts that increase our isola-tion in digital echo chambers and that amplify these toxic behaviors on levels not seen before. He suggests that there are also counter signs across the planet that people can respond to problems by opening the mind, heart, and will (through curiosity, compassion, and courage) instead of closing these capacities (through ignorance, hate, and fear).

The fall of Rome was followed by The Dark Ages, but The Way led into deserts where new experiments of the Spirit took place. These led to a Golden Age. Unless a significant number of people adopt a sustainable way of life today it seems likely that millions will die of plague, civil breakdown, and hunger. If this catastrophe takes place, those who have adopted a way of simplicity, discipline, and sustainable habits will be the survivors

Robin Mowat, the Oxford historian, wrote a series of books on the rise and fall of civilisations. Inspired by the historian Arnold Toynbee, Mowat believed that renewal in history was normally brought about by the influ-ence of creative minorities.

Arthur W. Schlesinger Jr. wrote "The problem of class is this: class conflict is essential if freedom is to be preserved, because it is the only bar-rier against class domination; yet class conflict, pursued to excess, may well destroy the underlaying fabric of common principle which sustains free society."[33] In the 2020s overlooked classes are rising up against the out-of-touch elites who fund their election to political parties of Right or Left. This revolt against the idea that 1 percent of people should control 99 percent of the money and community life of the people may be seen as an imprint of the Creator.

The prophet Isaiah understood how frequent and endemic were his people's conflating of national selfishness with God's will. He called them to look to the quarry from which they were mined (Isaiah 51:1). Penitent Westerners who want to repent of bad things in their society and learn

---

33. Schlesinger Jr., *Vital Center*

lessons from peoples who are closer to the earth cannot become Indians or Aborigines. There is, however, a forgotten treasure in the West that, if it is mined once again, can bring gleams of light and a flow of healing.

Brian Zahnd, lead pastor of Word of Life Church in St. Joseph, Missouri, had a mid-life crisis, and lost his appetite for "the mass-produced soda-like Christianity of North America". He read Dallas Willard's *The Divine Conspiracy*,[34] began to read the early church fathers and authors from a wide range of Christian traditions. He ceased to cast God and the Bible in his inherited image. He cast off his Western Christian idols and began to see how connected he was to all creation. He writes "Humanity did not come from somewhere other than the earth. Humanity's only home has been the spinning blue orb third from the sun. If this world is not our home (as the Gnostics claim) then we are homeless. We have a native connectedness to this creation that cannot be severed without suffering ill consequences. We are indigenous to the dirt. We are humans from the humus. We are a mysterious synthesis of the dust of the earth and the breath of God. To be too separated from unmolested nature tends towards a pathology of the soul."[35]

Charles Causley, a Cornish poet who died in 2003 put into words the heart cry of God to western churches:

> I am the great sun, but you do not see me,
> I am your husband, but you turn away.
> I am the captive, but you do not free me,
> I am the captain, but you will not obey.
> I am the truth, but you will not believe me,
> I am the city where you will not stay.
> I am your wife, your child, but you will leave me,
> I am that God to whom you will not pray.
> I am your counsel, but you will not hear me,
> I am your lover whom you will betray.
> I am your life, but if you will not name me,
> Seal up your soul with tears, and never blame me.

Karl Rahner predicted that "the devout Christian of the future will be either a mystic or will cease to be anything at all" Some White Christians who are suffocating in their own waste hear the Still Small Voice beneath and beyond the waste.

---

34. Willard, *Divine Conspiracy*.
35. Zahnd, *Water to Wine*

4

The Celtic Way

THE WAY OF CHRIST first spread among the Jews, then to the Greek-speaking people in the Roman Empire as described in The Acts of the Apostles. After that it spread to the Celtic peoples who were on the fringes of that empire, or outside it as in Ireland. Legends, admittedly late, say that Joseph of Arimathea planted a thorn tree at Glastonbury as a reminder of Jesus's crown of thorns. The stories of Jesus reached Britain when parts of it were still occupied by the Roman Empire. African and European units of the Roman Empire were stationed in Britain until 410. They had many religions, and some spread knowledge of Jesus. After the troops left, this knowledge was faint but revived through traders and immigrants who brought news of Egypt's desert fathers and mothers.

Celtic Christians were inspired by these "Athletes of Christ". They made ceaseless struggle to overcome what is not authentic—pride, lust, greed, envy for example until only the gentle love of God remained in them. Their earliest theologian, Pelagius, taught that the deepest reality about ourselves is not the ugliness of our sins but the beauty of our origins in God. Every human being has something in them of God's light that lights every person (John 1:4). God is the deepest part of our being. That is why we do not need to pretend or pressurize. We can be vulnerable in the presence of others and allow them to be who they are in our presence. We are available, but also we can be honest about our needs. Celtic Christianity takes sin seriously, but the sins we fight against are our false self, not our true self, which is made in God's image (Genesis 1:26).

Whereas missionaries on the continent of Europe cut down trees used at pagan centers of worship, there is no hint that missionaries to Celtic lands ever did this. They continued to honor the place given to trees by the indigenous population, and it seems the first church gatherings were held under large trees. When Germanus, Bishop of Auxerre, in Gaul, wrote a report of his visit to Britain, he describes a church meeting under leafy trees.[1]

We know that the ways of Jesus had taken deep root, because they had their own bishops. At the start of the seventh century colonial style Christianity was imposed on southern Britain when the Pope in Rome established an archbishop at Canterbury. Three indigenous Celtic bishops wondered whether they should co-operate with him or carry on in their own way. In order to discern God's will they sought out a hermit. Holiness, not hierarchy, was their highest source of authority. The hermit advised them that if the foreign archbishop was humble they should follow his advice, but if he was not humble they need not heed it. How would they know if he was humble, they asked? If he rose to greet them, thus treating them with dignity, they would know, the hermit replied. The archbishop did not rise to greet them.

In the central area of Britain British chiefs and landowners who had intermarried with Romans assumed leadership, after the Romans departed in 410, that sometimes transcended tribal boundaries. A revival of the Jesus movement was inspired not only by the Desert fathers and mothers, but also by the ascetic prayer lives of Europeans such as Martin of Tours who lived a simple life of prayer and agriculture with others in a building known as a White House. When he was made a bishop at Tours he refused to sit on a throne and asked for a cow stool instead. This inspired many people to adopt a Rule of Life and to become intoxicated with God. Numerous churches in Britain started as White Houses of prayer. Some grew into monastic villages that were marked by the gentle ways of Jesus. Ninian founded a famous white house at Whithorn (in today's Scotland), and Illtud at Llwantwit Major (in today's Wales).

Celtic Christians have a rapport with John the Loved Disciple, who perhaps more than any of the other apostles shows us how to have an authentic relationship with Jesus and with one another. They teach us to reflect upon the flowing love between John, the loved disciple, and Jesus, the gentle Lamb of God, that the tenderness of eternity be formed in our

---

1. Mayhew-Smith, *Naked Hermit.* 32

hearts. They inspire us to reflect on John listening to Jesus's heart-beat at the last supper and to the heart-beat of Jesus the Word in creation.

In Early Gaul

Irenaeus of the church of Celts in Lyons, a disciple of Bishop Polycarp who was mentored by the apostle John, taught that the Holy Spirit designed two essential means for the continuation of Jesus's mission on earth after his death. First, his message, continued through preachers, healers, and prophets directly inspired by God—the early ones became enshrined in the New Testament. Second, his embodiment through the universal church (the Body of Christ) held together by elders and bishops (overseers). The bishops/elders in council would discern which writings should be acknowledged by all Christians as Holy Scripture, and what is the mind of Christ on matters of doctrine or dispute. The bishop needs to discern the Spirit in people with charismatic callings, and they need to discern the Spirit in the bishop. The spontaneous charisms and the charism of the institution are the two arms of Christ. Even if we are not convinced by Irenaeus, we surely cannot dismiss the apostle Paul's criticism of Christians who split up into competing supporters of Cephas, or Apollos, or another leader (1 Corinthians 3:4).

In Ireland

Two thousand years ago Ireland had more than one hundred indigenous tribes. They had gods and spirits—good and bad. They had chiefs (or kings), foster mothers who were like elders, wise teachers named druids, and bards who sang or danced. They had prophets who foretold that greater light would come from the East, which they should accept. How would the Way of Jesus come to them?

One day a teenager in Britain who inherited a faint memory of Jesus from his parents, but who was aimless and without interest in it, was captured by Irish pirates while playing with his friends on the shore. His name was Patrick. The pirates sold him as a slave to a farmer in Ireland. In desperation Patrick turned to the God his forebears had believed in with all his heart. It was an experiment. He discovered that when he prayed hundreds of prayers through the freezing nights while he guarded sheep on the hills, he glowed inside and did not feel the cold. Then he discovered an inner voice. He assumed this was the voice of his forebears' God. After six years this voice told him to escape. He must walk miles along the shore until he saw a boat ready to sail across the sea, and he must offer the captain his wages if he would take him on board. Patrick got to what is now France, trained as a disciple of Jesus, learned the Bible and was ordained. He returned to his parents in Britain. They wanted him never to go far from them again, and to pastor a nearby church in a pleasant valley of roses. However, Patrick had a vision in the night. All the people of Ireland signed a letter to him. They implored him to walk among them once again and bring to them the ways of Jesus.

So, Patrick gathered a team and sailed into the river which you can see if you look down from a plane before it lands at Belfast airport. He had two advantages as a result of his time among the Irish as a slave: He already knew the language, and he had a relationship with the tribes who would look upon him as their adopted son.

Patrick started at the bottom, as a slave. Following his liberation and conversion to Christ he stayed at the bottom because in his heart he was the adopted child of the indigenous people of Ireland.

If he had a mission blueprint, he soon put this aside and followed Jesus's advice to his missionaries to go where they were invited. As daylight faded on their first day his team asked a farmer if he would, in accordance with the best tribal custom, give them accommodation. At first the farmer thought they had come to steal and had a knife ready to kill them. But when he looked into Patrick's face he saw only goodness and they became friends. They shared their stories, were invited to stay longer, and befriended the farmer's relatives and workers, who became followers of Jesus. They became perhaps the first church community in northern Ireland.

Patrick's team made friends like this with many tribes. The way of Jesus spread fast. But the chiefs and elders did not want their beliefs and ceremonies to be swept away as having no value. Patrick understood this. Their gods and spirits were married to the land, and he helped them to see that such a relationship could continue with the Creator. When they looked to the sun as a god whose favor they needed in order to bless their crops, Patrick kept respect for the sun central but extended it. He taught them that the sun was created by Jesus, whom he named the True, Uncreated Sun. Every time they looked at the created sun it could remind them of the Creator of the sun. They could still walk sun-wise with circling prayers, and they would pray to Jesus in the rhythms of the sun. Their great symbol would be a sun circling the cross of Jesus.

Patrick knew how to capture the imagination of the tribes. Each Spring solstice the High King of all the kings climbed the great Tara Hill with his horsed warriors and druids and lit a great fire to invoke the Sun to give them good crops in the coming season. On that day no one else in all Ireland could light a fire. Patrick, however, climbed the Hill of Slane, opposite, with his team and lit a fire to celebrate the rising from death of Jesus, the True Sun. "If you don't put that fire out this day", the Druid told the King, "the fire of this new faith will burn forever in our land". The High King sent his warriors to arrest Patrick's company. But they, too were warriors in spirit. They chanted "putting on armor prayers" and psalms such as *"Some trust in chariots and some trust in horses but we will trust in the Lord our God"* (Psalm 20:7). The tribes admired their shamans who could adopt strong animal personas. So, when a mist descended, and the warriors saw only deer running downhill, they were in awe of the shamans of Jesus.

One of the putting-on-armor prayers, or loricas, has come down to us. It is known as Saint Patrick's Breastplate. It tells us that the Creator has a force-field far greater than anything in films like Star Wars. It is also known as The Deer's Cry. You can guess why. The following is from Kuno Meyer's translation:

> I arise today
> Through a mighty strength, the invocation of the Trinity,
> Through belief in the threeness,
> Through confession of the oneness
> Of the Creator of Creation.
>
> I arise today . . .
> I arise today
> Through the strength of heaven;
> Light of sun,
> Radiance of moon,
> Splendour of fire,
> Speed of lightning,
> Swiftness of wind,
> Depth of sea,
> Stability of earth,
> Firmness of rock . . .
>
> Christ to shield me today,

Against poisoning, against burning,
Against drowning, against wounding,
So there come to me abundance of reward.

Christ with me, Christ before me, Christ behind me,
Christ in me, Christ beneath me, Christ above me,
Christ on my right, Christ on my left,
Christ when I lie down, Christ when I sit down,
Christ when I arise, Christ in the heart of every man who thinks of me,
Christ in the mouth of every one who speaks of me,
Christ in the eye of every one who sees me,
Christ in every ear that hears me.[2]

As well as prayers Patrick taught the Irish to recite attributes of the Creator. Although the Spirit of Jesus inside him inspired him, he always remembered that the followers of Jesus throughout the world were like one large scattered tribe, which had certain ceremonies and sayings in common. One of these, which he had learned when he trained as a priest in France, was called The Creed. Patrick was loyal to the big Jesus tribe's creed, but he felt it was dry and "did not scratch where the Irish itched". So he filled it out. That is why when they recited Patrick's Creed they spoke of the living Creator of the rivers and mountains, who brings breath to every being and lives in their bodies.

Patrick gathered the big chief Laeghaire, the chief Bard, and the law-makers of his part of Ireland. They set out the laws of Ireland. These laws are known as the Senchus Mor. It seems that some were written down at that time but that most were handed down by word of mouth until the seventh century when Cenn Faelad wrote them down. We are told that Patrick gathered the leaders and preached Jesus's Gospel to them. Over the following months as they witnessed signs and miracles they bowed in obedience to God and Patrick. Big Chief Laeghaire and Patrick then gathered the poets, teachers, and law-makers and drew up the Laws of Ireland. A wise man named Dubtach set out all the legal judgements that prevailed through the law of nature, and the law of the seers, and in the judgements delivered, and through the poets. They had foretold that the bright word of blessing would come, for it was the Holy Spirit who spoke through the mouths of these pagan lovers of justice, for the law of nature had prevailed where the written law did not reach. Now they put together the true judgements that

2. Meyer, *Ancient Irish Poetry*.

the Holy Spirit had spoken through the law-makers and poets down to the reception of the Faith of Jesus. What did not clash with the Word of God in the Old and New Testaments, and with the consciences of believers, was confirmed in the law of the Brehons by Patrick and the church leaders and chiefs of Ireland. For the law of nature had been quite right, except for the additions of the faith and the church and its people.[3]

The Irish understood that God was calling them to become a country organized according to laws revealed by God, but these enhanced, rather than obliterated their existing laws:[4]

It was the Christian monks who wrote down all the favourite tribal stories and memories that the bards passed down. They treasured the spiritual heritage of their people.

Patrick "spoke truth to power". When a fellow Briton named Coroticus, who was a well-known Christian Chief, captured some of Patrick's Irish converts to sell as slaves, Patrick sent a priest with a letter to him and his soldiers. It included these words: "See how they have filled their houses with the spoils of dead Christians? Why, they devote their lives to plunder! Miserable men, they have no idea how they feed poison, food that surely kills, to their friends and even to their own children; just as Eve never realized that she was handing out certain death to her own man, her husband. What kind of hope can you have left in God? Can you still trust someone who says he agrees with you? Do you listen still to all those flatterers who surround you? God alone will judge . . ."

It was said that Patrick had a weekly meeting with his soul friend who was named Victor. People speculate as to whether this was his spirit guide (western tribes use the term angel) or whether it was an elder from what is now France whom Patrick invited over to be part of his team. Patrick wanted the Irish above all to have a love affair with God. How could he help them understand that the essence of Jesus, and the Father/Mother, and the Spirit who prayed inside them, were eternally communing in love? That love was their one essence, but the three expressions of love made God like a community into which we are invited. Legend says that he often displayed the three-leafed shamrock. "Three in one and One in Three, God is our Community".

In his auto-biographical Confession of Faith, Patrick writes:

3. Stubbs et al, *Councils and Ecclesiastical.*
4. Hancock, *Senchus Mor*

> I owe an immense debt to God, who granted me so much grace
> that many people in Ireland were reborn in God through me.
> Clergy were ordained everywhere to look after these people, who
> had come to trust the Lord who called them from the ends of the
> earth. It was essential that we spread our nets so that a great mul-
> titude should be taken for God.

Patrick led many to follow the Way of Christ, but it was not until a few generations after him that a whole stream of holy men and women founded monastic villages of God either within a tribe or that attracted people from varied tribes.

Finnian's monastic school at Clonard was situated by the river Boyne which divides south and north Ireland, by the Esker ridge, a key west-east route. It was a neutral place, open to all. Finnian performed miracles of faith but retained poverty of spirit. He began alone and lived in a simple cell of wattles and clay, built a little church and enclosed them. Like a magnet, many were attracted to live around a person of such holiness and scholarship. It was said that he trained "the twelve apostles of Ireland". These included Cieran of Clonmacnoise, Columba of Iona, and Brendan of Clonfert. All these apostles went out to found monasteries and schools that were famed throughout Europe. The teaching was all by word of mouth, and the students built their own little huts in the surrounding meadows where they fished and milled their grain. Monks spent hours with their hands spread in prayer, in study of Scripture, and in manual labour.

Bangor monastery was established by St. Comgall in 558. Bernard of Clairvaux called it a valley off angels, and it trained many missionaries.

Brendan was born in AD 484 in Banna, near Ardfert, not far from Tralee in County Kerry in the south-west of Ireland. Brendan's people belonged to the Altraige tribe. On the night of his birth the local bishop, Erc, saw the village in one great blaze of light, with angels shining around it. Realising that this child was destined for some special calling he asked a nun called Ita to educate Brendan as his spiritual foster mother Some distance from Ardfert is Wether's Well (Tobar na Molt) in which Brendan was baptized by Bishop Erc. It is a significant pilgrimage site.

At the age of twenty-six, Brendan was ordained a priest and founded a number of monasteries. Brendan's first voyage took him to the Aran Islands, where he founded a monastery. Between AD 512 and 530 Brendan built monastic cells at Ardfert, and Shanakee at the foot of Mount Brandon. This looked out on to the Atlantic Ocean which provided a highway for traders and travelers. Jesus's disciples in Ireland looked for a wilderness where they might be alone with God. They called the Atlantic their wilderness, and many also set out to experience God in this wilderness. They were traveling between two worlds. They were known as pilgrims, which meant they were open to a spirit which can affect people in different ways. Many pilgrims carry "baggage", but Brendan had to shed baggage.

From there he is supposed to have embarked on his famous voyage of seven years in search of Paradise, which ended in America. As the stories of the seven years voyage spread, crowds of pilgrims and students flocked to Ardfert. Religious houses were formed at Gallarus, Kilmalchedor, Brandon Hill, and Inistooskert in the Blasket Islands, in order to meet the wants of those who came for spiritual guidance. At the United States Naval Academy in Annapolis, Maryland, a large stained-glass window commemorates Brendan's achievements.

Following his return to Ireland he founded a monastery in Annaghdown, where he spent the rest of his life, and a convent at Annaghdown for his sister Briga. Fearing that after his death his devotees might take his remains as relics, Brendan had previously arranged to have his body secretly returned to the monastery he founded in Clonfert, concealed in a luggage cart. It was said there were three thousand brothers at Clonfert on the site of the present Clonfert Cathedral. He called this his "place of resurrection".

Adomnan's Life of Columba tells how he founded many cells and monastic villages. It refers to him going inside to a building only when they received the bread and wine—it seems that before that their worship was outside.[5] Columba forbade sacred oak trees to be cut down even for the building of a new monastery.

A young carpenter named Ciaran received guidance in a prophecy that a tree planted by the River Shannon would bear fruit for all Ireland. Ciaran established a monastery at Clonmacnoise; this was by the River Shannon and an esker ridge which connected Ireland east to west. It is said that the two tribes each side of this area were hostile towards one another, but Ciaran's monastery brought them together. It lasted a thousand years and bore great fruit in holy lives, learning, hospitality, crops, and crafts. Today believers are inspired by Ciaran to a ministry of healing wounded memory.

Ireland became a land of hospitality. This aspect of the Jesus Way came especially through the spiritual mothers. A little girl named Brigid heard Patrick preach not long before he died. Her father was a pagan chief but her

---

5. Sharpe, *Life of St. Columba.*

mother, when she followed Jesus, was sent to work as a Druid's slave. Brigid taught people to lay a spare place at every meal table in case Jesus came in the guise of a needy visitor.

She established a large monastic community for women and men at Kildare, in the Center of Ireland. It provided barrels of apples and ale for pilgrims and poor people. The sisters kept a fire alight night and day for a thousand years. Her many small communities became sanctuaries that replaced the forts as Ireland's centers of influence. She encouraged people to have an Anamcara—a soul friend. "A person without a soul friend is like a body without a head" she taught. She also taught everyone to bless people. Even today, the Irish Tourist Board has posters which welcome visitors with the words in Gaelic and English "A hundred thousand welcomes". Celtic Christians blessed "every blessed thing", in kitchens, work places, in nature and in key life events.

Irish Celts had chiefs, wise teaching elders called druids, and poets who sang and sometimes danced called bards. After they followed Jesus one of the chief's children often became the spiritual papa or mama of the church villages that became the tribal hub. The druids were still respected. The saintly Columba said that he asked Jesus to be his druid. The druids gradually merged with the new church village teachers. Chiefs held ceremonies to celebrate each season. These might include dance, sport, singing, and bards would keep the tribal memory alive by reciting or singing of past events. When a whole tribe followed the ways of Jesus they still honored the bards. Adult monks as well as children were part of a residential school. They copied down the old tribal stories and re-told them. Parts of the twelfth century Book of Leinster were copied earlier in the Irish monastery at Tallagh, now a suburb of Dublin. This tells us that the monks soaked themselves in the poems and stories of the traditional bards. The bardic tradition was like a cow that never grows dry.[6]

Like Indian and Bible tribes, pre-Christian Celtic tribes had prophecies. They had heard of an eclipse of the sun and an earth quake in the first century. Later they learned about the death and resurrection of Jesus. A legend grew that when their High King asked his Druid what the meaning of these portents of nature was, the Druid replied that they were signs that far away the Son of the High King of all the world had been nailed to death on a cross of wood placed in the earth. Even if this story was put together later, it tells us that Celtic followers of Jesus recognized that their

6. Flower, *Irish Tradition*.

tribes had had prophets who prepared their people to welcome a greater light that was coming.

When warriors and farm workers became monks consecrated to Jesus alone, they showed that they were monks by wearing a uniform called a habit and by cutting off their hair at the front like monks throughout the world. But they continued to honor their tribal ways by letting their hair grow long at the back. Later they were told by colonial style church leaders that they must cut off their hair at the back also. This was a similar approach to that taken by USA missionaries in government and church-sponsored schools: they cut the hair of Native boys and girls in a uniform style up until the 1990s.

Many tribes have ceremonies when they remember or make contact with the ancestors. The Celtic tribes did this at the start of their season of dark which began on November 1 (Samhain). Darkness brings fears to the surface. Family members who died with a grudge against them might haunt them. So, in these ceremonies they honored the dead by keeping memories alive and they tried to quieten the dead by encircling themselves with fire and smoke. When these tribes followed Jesus, they realized that these issues still existed, but they had more light than before. They continued holding a ceremony at this time but instead of focusing on the fears, they focused on Jesus, the one Person who could be a true mediator between the unhappy dead forebears and themselves—and especially on holy role models who had glowed with the eternal life of Jesus when they died. The wider Christian church also adopted this practice. Nowadays they call November 1 All Saints Day, and the evening before is preparing for this hallowing, or making holy, which is the true meaning of Halloween. Although in the secular West Halloween has become debased and commercialized, some churches still light fires or candles. In my church we held children's Angel parties on this night. The Community of Aidan and Hilda has a Halloween prayer service for the honoring of forebears.[7]

So the people of Ireland fell in love with God and became a land of saints and scholars.

England

Through Patrick and others, certain British tribes had helped to bring the Way of Jesus to Ireland.

7. Simpson, *Liturgies from Lindisfarne.*

Then a disaster overtook central Britain. It was as bad as the near genocide or cruel colonization of the American tribes by the European invaders. Fierce invaders from Germanic tribes captured the forts of Celtic tribes, slew their leaders and land owners, and created kingdoms instead of tribes. They were called Angles and Saxons. When eventually these colonial kingdoms merged, they became Britain's first nation state (England) and the world's first English-speaking people. Their descendants are still known as "the Anglo-Saxon world". Though they could make good quality artefacts, they did not know Jesus and they could be brutal. The men would fight battles in summer, and booze and brag about their exploits in winter. The poor women had to do the menial work, look after the children, and often lose their husband on the killing fields. Their kings slew one another. Their sons, the rightful heirs, would be slain or seek sanctuary with a neighboring tribe. Could it be possible that the Creator would seek a way to change even these hard-hearted peoples?

One such royal son, Oswald, was given sanctuary by an Irish tribe which had settled in what is now Argyll in Scotland. This tribe followed Jesus's ways. The great Columba had founded his monastic village in it, on the island of Iona. Oswald, a fine warrior, became a friend of Jesus. In time he regained his rightful role as King of the largest Anglo-Saxon kingdom, Northumbria, which spanned today's northern England and southern Scotland. He asked Iona to send a mission to help his people welcome Jesus into their hearts. His people included the Anglo-Saxons, and the remnants of Pictish, Britonnic, and Irish Scots tribes.

The first missionary Iona sent failed. He behaved like a colonist. He expected the people to come to his base. He had not learned their language so he needed a translator. If they accepted his teaching, they had to leave their own village and go to a foreign building called a church for a ceremony that had nothing in common with their everyday lives. The leader of that mission returned to Iona. He explained it was a failure because the people were barbarians. He thought barbarians were too uncivilized to become Christians.

This was a deep disappointment, so the Iona elders held a council. What had they got wrong? What did they need to learn? A monk named Aidan perhaps thought of his Irish tribes, where Jesus was welcomed into their natural patterns. He said that a missionary should not require someone who follows Jesus to accept the foreign culture of the missionary's tribe, or even of their own ruler if it meant breaking up their village community life. A mother gives milk from her own breast which flows into her children. Missionaries should be like those mothers—embrace those dear people as if they are family and give them the milk of Jesus's words and kindness before giving them the meat.

Aidan's words so touched the hearts of the Iona brothers that they sent him on a second, "last chance" mission. Like Jesus with his twelve apostles, Aidan took twelve brothers with him. At first, they had to work on the Anglo-Saxon language. They could probably be understood by the peasant Celtic remnants in the west and north of Northumbria.

Aidan had three rules for his missionary brothers: 1) Walk among the people and make friends. 2) Accept invitations to visit their homes and share stories. 3) Store the Gospel stories of Jesus in their hearts so that they shared living words, not a book. King Oswald offered Aidan a royal horse so that, in the fashion of modern western missions, he could reach the greatest number of people in the shortest possible time. Aidan, risking the king's anger, refused it because he knew that only rich people could afford horses, and he did not want to be above people. He also wanted to spend time with the people and be on a level with them.

Aidan had two other great principles: the brothers must model Jesus's ways in their personal lives, and model villages that reflected Jesus in their daily patterns of prayer, learning, farming, arts, and hospitality. Anglo-Saxon people would become equal partners in these villages. Aidan's aim was to grow an indigenous church for English-speaking people.[8]

If rich people gave Aidan money to influence him, he would give it to the poor, and spend none of it on church buildings, which were simple and made of wood. Sometimes he would go to a slave market and buy a slave his freedom, perhaps offering him a job in one of his model villages. He and his brothers were so tender hearted that people would run out of their villages to greet them and ask them to pray for them and their children.

Aidan, like Patrick, had a love for the poor and spoke truth to power. A black theologian named Robert Beckford was a presenter in a six-part TV series on the History of Christianity. One part focused on Aidan's Irish Mission. Beckford said that although he was committed to Christ, he had always been ambivalent about how Christianity had failed to apply Christ's ways. For example, his American grandparents had worked for slave own-ers who made sure the Gospel was preached but they modeled slavery. Now,

---

8. Simpson and Lyons Lee, *St. Aidan's Way.*

however, that he had learned of Aidan's much earlier and more authentic model, he could be wholehearted about Christianity.

Aidan's first monastic village was on the tidal island of Lindisfarne. At high tide they could sustain a contemplative spirit: at low tide the world could come to them and they could go out to the world. After Aidan's death this monastery produced the beautifully illustrated Lindisfarne Gospels, whose artwork embraced Saxon, Irish, Coptic, European, Oriental, and Byzantine styles. A translation from the Latin which a Durham monk later scribbled in the margins is the world's first example of the English language.

Soon there were monastic villages of God in many other places. The ways of Jesus spread fast, even after Oswald was killed and two sub-kingdoms jostled for power. The King of the smaller, southern sub kingdom befriended Aidan and gave him his most expensive horse, because of Aidan's long hazardous journeys and advancing age. When Aidan met a beggar he gave him the horse! The furious King exploded in anger. "Which is more precious to you, that child of a mare (a mother horse) or that child of God?" asked Aidan, thus declaring the value of every human life. The king's heart changed and he asked forgiveness.

There is an advertisement for a beer which says "it reaches the parts others cannot reach". I think Aidan realized there were parts of the Anglo-Saxon character that only women could reach. Ireland had her spiritual mothers: he must establish them among the English. That was a huge challenge. The key person who made this possible was Princess Hilda. Her pagan parents came from a minority Anglo-Saxon tribe that was used to fighting battles and losing them. Her father fled from attackers and died while she was in her mother's womb. Her anguished mother had a dream. She searched within the folds of her cloak and found a jewel. It was so brilliant that it lit up all the indigenous and settler tribes of the British Isles. This reminds us that the Creator can speak to people through dreams whatever are their gods. People realized later that Hilda was that jewel.

She had become a Christian as a girl during a short-lived Roman mission, but when she met Aidan she was captivated by his Irish spirituality and embraced it with all her heart. He recalled her from exile to establish a women's monastic village near the River Wear, then she led a monastic community for men and women at Hartlepool famed for its integrity, justice, and holistic learning.

After Aidan's death she headed the largest English monastic village for men and women at Whitby. There, she recognized a vocation in an illiterate cow-herd named Caedmon. His name is Celtic. She had him taught Bible stories which he turned into the first pop songs in English. Those inspired by her today seek to "release the song in every human heart". I was a guest of students in Texas who were playing football. There was just one black student who, feeling marginalized, began to walk away. I learned he studied music, and told him the story of Caedmon. Thirty minutes later he returned. "Could you repeat what you said to me?" he asked. "You can release the song in every human heart" I told him.

Hilda was treasured as "a merciful mother" by people of conflicting traditions from far and wide, and inspired countless vocations. Never again, anywhere in Christendom, for thirteen hundred years, would a woman be a spiritual mother of such a large community of both women and men.[9]

Although the Irish monks at Lindisfarne returned to their homeland after the king commanded the church to hold a synod in 664 which replaced Celtic with Roman ways, a cross-cultural transfusion had taken place which enabled something of the Celtic spirit to continue under the new "colonial" framework.

A shining example of this is the night of Aidan's death at Bamburgh on 31 August 661. Forty miles north a young Anglo-Saxon warrior named Cuthbert was on military duty guarding sheep at night when he saw a holy soul being escorted to heaven. He vowed that when his term of duty expired he would offer himself for life monastic service in the English church. He became a great healer, soul friend, overseer, and missionary church planter who, in life and death, inspired large numbers to holy living. Once he stood in the sea all night seeking cleansing for a monastic village which had developed bad habits. All sorts of people confided in him and he wept for them.

The Lindisfarne Gospels, are dedicated to God and Saint Cuthbert. They are beautifully inscribed, and the pages are decorated with animal figures in many bright colors. When I showed pilgrims from Canada around the Lindisfarne Gospels Center on England's Holy Island of Lindisfarne they exclaimed that the zoomorphic, intertwined animal designs around the page edges reminded them of the art of some of their indigenous peoples.

Eadfrith, the main scribe, made a deliberate mistake. He did not want to draw praise for himself, he wanted God to get all the glory. The Navajo also believe that a work of art should not be perfect. If they make a rug they

9. Simpson, *Hilda of Whitby*.

will deliberately make one thread go from its pattern to the outer border. Both Celtics and Indians know that the proud person resists their Creator and does not breathe spiritually (Psalm 3:34 and Isaiah 4:6).

The area of Britain colonized by the Anglo-Saxons became known as England. The best historian of those days, a monk named Bede, concluded that the Gospel of Jesus, as brought by Aidan's Irish mission, had united four previously warring tribes, who each spoke a different language: Picts, Scots, Britons, and English.

The *Life of Cuthbert* by an anonymous monk of Lindisfarne, Bede's *Life* and the hermit Guthlac's hagiographer Felix all tell of hermits who enjoyed a special relationship with the elements, birds, and animals. Nick Mayhew-Smith,[10] suggests it was this relationship with nature that led Bede to write his theological formula about our "lost dominion" over creation. Bede writes in his *Life* of Cuthbert "For if a man faithfully and wholeheartedly serves the maker of all created things, it is no wonder that all creation should minister to his commands and wishes".

Felix added two of his own reasons why nature rituals were important: because a true Christian is united with every other creature in communion with God and because this is a way to meet with the angels.

Nick Mayhew-Smith argues that the vision of the early Celtic church was to restore communion with creation which they often picture as restoring Eden. The mythical voyages in the Brendan genre were often to discover an Eden or paradise where the original blessed creation could be re-instituted. Bishop Athanasius taught that when Christ immersed himself in the river Jordan, he was inaugurating a new creation by re-uniting it as well as all humanity with God. Mayhew-Smith links the Celtic practice of open-air baptisms and regular prayer while submerged in water as a spiritual practice that helped to restore this communion of our bodies and souls with God in creation. This concept was taught by Saint John Chrysostom: he suggests that baptism is a bodily recreation, akin to the making of Adam out of earth. Mayhew-Smith links the story of Germanus calming the seas by sprinkling oil on them, with Columba's calming of Lough Ness and its monster and Aidan telling the future queen's escort to sprinkle blessed oil on the troubled waters with a redeeming of creation, and he quotes a poem *In Praise of Columcille* which says "It was not on soft beds he undertook elaborate prayers, he crucified—it was not for crimes—his body on the green waves."

10. Mayhew-Smith, *Naked Hermit.*

Cuthbert's actions frequently ended up having a participatory effect on the environment. After he prayed all night in the sea at Coldingham creation is so moved that it sends two otters to warm his feet. On Epiphany, while evangelizing among the Picts, St. Cuthbert's party is stranded upon the shore by a storm but the seas casts up provisions in the form of dolphin meat that tastes like honey. In the Teviot hills Cuthbert prophecies to a boy he is mentoring that an eagle they see flying overhead will bring their meal. It duly deposits a fish, but Cuthbert tells his companion to give some of the fish to the bird, because he interprets the bird's behaviour as "fasting".

Perhaps the most memorable example of how a tribe can introduce the ways of Jesus to a colonial oppressor and transform the brutal roots of its culture is expressed in an Anglo-Saxon poem called *The Dream of the Rood*. The Rood is the Tree on which Jesus was crucified (1 Peter 2:24). Aidan's Celtic Mission had introduced the idea that the Tree of Death could become the Tree of Life, and this poem is one of its fruits. In this poem Jesus becomes an Anglo-Saxon warrior who leaps lithely on to the Cross to redeem human kind—not by oppression or killing: the "weapon" is total self-giving. Is this a clue as to how Native tribes can, against all odds, redeem the white tribes who colonize and fragment, blindly mis-using the name of the Savior of the world? The whip hand of Euro-America that splinters all it touches can become the tender hand that heals a splintered world.

Villages of God

In many tribal villages (pueblos in New Mexico, mesas among the Hopi) a church has been added. It may be physically on the edge and it is often culturally apart. However, early churches in Ireland and then in Britain were unlike those in the Roman Empire; they reflected natural and tribal patterns in a "peoples" monasticism. Tribal leaders who were converted to Christ by evangelists or who welcomed the new faith gave prime estates, often by the strategic highways of sea and river, to outstanding Christians among their ruling families who took vows and established communities of daily prayer, education, hospitality, and land care. These "peoples monastery churches" served as daily prayer base, school, library, scriptorium/arts center, drop-in, library, school, health center. They had farms with livestock and crops, workshops such as wood, spinning and milling. They were open to the world. They offered soul friends, training, and even entertainment. Children, housewives, farm workers, and even a few animals would wander in and out. Visitors brought news from overseas. Each had its own flavor in worship and values (Rule) yet each was connected with the universal church through common practices, prayers, and priests ordained in the apostolic succession.

They developed praying spaces and learning spaces, guest spaces and eating spaces, spaces for crops and cattle, sewing and spinning, ceremonies and solitude, milling, and pottery, and art. They maintained daily prayer in the rhythms of the sun. All human life flourished there. Children could play and the old could stay. The church was the heart of the tribe.

Studies have shown that a wide swathe of Eurasia shared, through trading sea routes, some non-Roman influences that emphasized such a simpler, more communal and organic way of following Jesus. This included Coptic monks and Middle East peoples, and the Celtic Arc from Armenia and Turkey to Europe's western shores.[11]

From Ireland missionaries and theologians turned Europe's Dark Age into a new Golden Age.

Sadly, the Celtic ways were replaced by the ways of the church in mainland Europe which had been shaped by a colonial form of mission. The Roman Empire had an emperor at the top, and subordinates who ruled administrative areas in a top-down way. This was efficient but did not grow out of local relationships. This Roman way of organizing the church was gradually imposed upon Celtic lands. I have mentioned that monks were required to cut off their long hair. But the greater losses were to do with relationship—with creation, with their natural communities, and with the Triune source of community.

Vikings overran Lindisfarne in 793. In 1066 Normans from France became England's rulers, introducing the feudal class system and belittling the role of women. The religious Reformation gave individuals a chance to read the Bible and follow their consciences, but it did not restore those relationships that had been lost. In Ireland in the twelfth century the monastic villages were replaced by the Roman system of dioceses.

The Celtic tribes had been marginalized and assimilated. Native American people have also suffered terribly from migrants from Europe who mis-used the land and its peoples. Those of us who were on Europe's western fringes have suffered over a longer period from migrants who invaded us from other lands, but with hindsight we can see that they brought something positive as well as bad things. The Romans invaded—but they

11. Ghazarian, *Mediterranean Legacy.*

gave us warm baths. The Anglo-Saxons invaded—but they gave us schools. The Vikings invaded—but they gave us good ways of farming. The French Normans invaded—but they gave us good buildings. Africans, Asians, Muslims have occupied our spaces, they give us music, joy, and prayer.

Jesus invited us to pray "Your kingdom come on earth", not because he was a colonial invader but because he became indigenous. In those days the Jews model of glory days was of a good and great king. So, Jesus invited them to have something much better—a Servant King who makes every person royal as they find their God-given calling in life.

After the Norman, Viking and Anglo-Saxon invasions, the Celtic river had become but a few underground streams. However, in recent times those streams have surfaced again. The cry of peoples who are tired of top-down societies and colonial types of church, who yearn for community and know they are connected to the earth, who no longer believe in a God made in the image of empire can no longer be stifled. That is why a new way for the West is possible.

Celtic High Crosses

Stone High Crosses in Britain began in the seventh century, but the panels of iconography on ninth century Irish Crosses have an unparalleled richness. They have been described as Ireland's greatest contribution to the sculpture of medieval Europe. The best examples are sited at the monastic sites of Monasterboice and Clonmacnoise (with their Scripture Crosses)— as well as the site of the Irish monastery at Iona in Scotland.

In an age when few could read, it seems those responsible for the crosses wanted to re-tell biblical stories. Rather like comics today, these selections from both the Old and New Testaments point to a particular truth.

The two large arms are centered around a large ring or circle. The purpose of the circle was both practical and philosophical. The circle gave structural support to the two arms; without the circle these cross-pieces easily came apart but symbolically the cruciform shape is central. But there is much more than that. Christ was crucified on a cross. The circle, or ring, is also a symbol of the cosmos. The prevalence of figures of Adam and Eve on these crosses is no accident. The cross proclaimed that the sin of Eden leading to the fall of humans and creation was reversed. A new creation was being proclaimed.

Roots and Fruits

The future grows out of the past, so we need to keep alive a memory of our roots. For those with Celtic roots, our past, for all its schisms and betrayals, is rooted in belief in God. The value of that belief is questioned today by new atheists and by well-meaning people who think that religion has stifled human rights and has fostered intolerance. They forget that religion has prophets as well as prelates, that churches point us away from themselves to God and the common good, and that the seeds of corruption lie within us all. Societies are doomed to a downward spiral of rottenness unless the deepest emotional springs of their people are rooted in an I-you relationship that brings well-being. The great Faiths believe that families are essential building blocks of civilisation and that the Family of Humankind becomes a mirage without a sense that all are children of a Divine "Parent".

When Christianity brought to pagan Ireland a written language, the Irish fell in love both with Jesus and with the laws that God gave Moses in order to create a good society. The Brehon laws reflect much in the Old Testament, for there were similarities in context at that time. Contexts change, but not the underlying values. 800 years after Moses, the prophet Jeremiah realized his country faced a turning point, and he acted out an unforgettable message. He bought new skin-close clothes for all to see. While they were still fresh, he hid them under some dusty rocks. Later, he recovered them. The clothes had disintegrated and were good for nothing. The point was: the secret of his people's greatness was to stay as close to God as those clothes were to him. Because they had instead become arrogant and selfish, and behaved as if they were self-made, they would become good for nothing and find themselves discarded.

Celtic Christianity Today

I joke to USA pilgrims to Lindisfarne that the original WASPS were converted to Christ in that place. The WASPS were White Anglo-Saxon Pagans. The supreme value they learned from Christ's missionaries was not to trample down others, but to lay down their lives in sacrifice.

The Celtic Christian tradition combines a beautiful spontaneity that allows each person to be guided by the Holy Spirit with a beautiful community that calls us to obedience, that is attentive listening to and honoring of others. We strive to weave together the God-given strands in Christianity which have become separated, for example the Pentecostal, Scriptural, Sacramental, Contemplative, and Social Service strands.

A growing number seek to rediscover a dynamic from their own ancient indigenous Celtic tribes, to draw living water from these ancient wellsprings, and to learn from them how our societies may follow better ways. US pastor Kenneth Macintosh, who has written *Water from an Ancient Well: Celtic Spirituality for Modern Life* (Anamchara Books) is one of this number. He writes of these early followers of Jesus: "They were tribal people, deeply rooted in their lands, and their faith remained close to the soil, the mountains, the lakes, and sky. Like the knotwork patterns they loved, they believed spirituality was inseparably woven into life's every aspect". Through "pilgrims for the love of God" such as Columbanus they influenced much of Europe for centuries, until non-tribal ways of ordering church and society took over.

In Australia David Tacey's book *Re-enchantment: New Australian Spirituality* points out that the power of the land and the influence of aboriginal culture are activating primordial levels of the Euro-Australian psyche, stirring its deeper layers. Tacey believes that a version of ancient Celtic spirituality is being awakened and stirred to new life in Australia. One can see many signs of this in Australian folk culture, where the attempt to "grow down" into Australian soil has the effect of revitalizing Celtic roots, giving rise to a redeeming of primal roots through Christ.[12]

Those who draw water from these well-springs become part of a back-to-the-future movement. They are like the scribe Jesus commended because he took the best of the old and the new from God's treasury. They heed the timeless call of the prophet Jeremiah *"Stand at the cross roads and follow the ancient paths."* Jeremiah 6:16.

Although the Irish and British tribes died out as distinct entities, I liken their spirituality, in my book *Exploring Celtic Spirituality: ancient roots for our future*,[13] to a river that went underground but is now re-surfacing in a different terrain.

Timothy Joyce[14] writes that the Celts "are recognized as the "European Aborigines," like Native American tribes already on the land with their own developed culture prior to being conquered, driven out, or assimilated by more powerful invaders". Alastair McIntosh, a Scottish activist and scholar,

---

12. Lyons Lee and Simpson, *Celtic Spirituality.*

13. Simpson, *Celtic Christianity.*

14 Joyce, *Celtic Christianity.*

reports similar instances of identification between modern Scottish activists and Native North Americans. After viewing a television program on Native Americans, Torcuil MacRath, an elderly friend of McIntosh's, commented, "they said that their culture is dying. They said it's because the Circle, the Sacred Hoop, has been broken . . . It's the same for us. It's the same for the Gael . . . Because when I heard them on the television, those Indians, I understood instantly what they meant."[15] Interestingly, Sulian Stone Eagle Herney, a Mi'Kmaq activist brought to Scotland by McIntosh, recognized this indigenous connection as well. While visiting a community development project in Glasgow, Stone Eagle said, "your situation is the same as ours," referring to the inner-city poverty and dislocation of the Scottish people. The idea of "Celticity" provides a sense of roots for modern, industrialized individuals who might feel separated from their cultural heritage. This argument for indigenousness often includes the story of the oppression of the Celtic tradition by the powerful forces of both Rome and the Protestant British. For many, Celtic spirituality is an expression of Christianity that will survive the top-down models of the fading Christendom era. Even though we live in a post-tribal society connected up through trade and internet, this "back to basics" movement is about ways of "seeing", praying and relating to people and creation that can start in our hearts and extend to networks and communities. First Nation peoples, disillusioned westerners, and spiritually thirsty people in all continents want to drink from this river.

Five marks of resurgent Celtic spirituality are:

1. Roots in Scripture, the Spirit and the Soil.
2. Rhythms of daily and seasonal prayer, work and re-creation.
3. Relationships with soul friends and communities.
4. Pilgrimage, awareness and blessing.
5. Churches as holistic hubs with a heart for God, others and the world.

Commenting on the prologue to John's Gospel, J. Philip Newell, a Canadian who is a former warden at Iona Abbey, observes[16] that "John is listening to the universe as an expression of God. It is spoken into being by the One from whom all things come. It comes directly from the heart of God's being. And in it we can hear the sound of the one Heartbeat. The

15. McIntosh, *Hell and High Water*.
16. Newell, *Christ of the Celts*.

whiteness of the moon, the wildness of the wind, the moisture of the fecund earth is the glow and whiteness and moistness of God now".

Modern new monastic communities inspired by the Celtic tradition use patterns of prayer that embrace ancient wisdoms. An Informal Celtic Communion begins "Let this wondrous creation, plundered by alien forces, open wide its arms to its returning Savior. Let all the people, marked by the Creator's dignity, welcome him who comes to restore our lost innocence."[17]

The possibility of "villages of God" emerging in the fluidity of modern western life is also gripping people's imagination. The American independent pastor Paul Sparks emphasizes how powerful the gospel can be when it takes root in the context of a place, at the intersection of geography, demography, economy, and culture. He acknowledges that his is not a new idea—the concept of a parish is as old as Paul's letters to the various communities of the ancient church—but in an age of dislocation and disengagement, the notion of a church that knows its place and gives itself to where it finds itself is like a breath of fresh air, like a sign of new life. He encourages people who drive to a church from elsewhere to take an interest in the neighborhood that surrounds the church building and to ask "what are the signs of God at work there?" These may include the witness of Christians from other churches, but also people of goodwill who run shops, clubs, services, and planning departments.[18]

Emerging villages of God typically start with a multi-facility church building that is a hub for a locality, but it grows through relationships with people of good will in the local community. Sooner or later spaces for praying and silence, art and education, ecology and socialising, cooking and guest accommodation, sport and leisure, recording and celebration become a safe sanctuary and a creative focus. They reflect a community more than a competitor. A virtual chart of ingredients in different villages of God is included in my High Street Monasteries: Fresh Expressions of Committed Christianity.[19] and is available as a download from my web site www.raysimpson.org

Much has been made of the fact that there is no evidence of early British or Irish missionaries chopping down sacred trees or pagan shrines, as was done on the continent. The fact that none were martyred is taken as a sign that they embraced their culture and the people embraced them and

---

17. Simpson, *Liturgies from Lindisfarne* 360.

18. Sparks et al, *New Parish*.

19. Simpson, *High Street Monasteries*

their new faith in varying degrees. We know that Saint Columba fought to retain the rights of bards in the emerging Christian society and that he called Christ his Druid. Perhaps the most compelling evidence for the indigenous principle is that a few generations after Saint Patrick's evangelisation much of the Irish church was in effect a village of the tribe.

Contemporary Celtic communities such as The Community of Aidan and Hilda promote the indigenous principle because it is right, not because certain groups followed it in a particular era. Its rationale derives from the incarnation of Christ in a particular culture.

We may fairly conclude that the incarnational principle is enshrined in Christianity, but has for long periods has not been practiced in the missions of the church. The promotion of indigenous church patterns is not exclusively Celtic, but the early Celtic churches do provide us with examples of it.

We cannot, of course, recreate the organization of the early Celtic church. But it is possible to learn from them, and it is necessary to draw lessons from the story of western churches. Although the Reformation threw out what was oppressive in church and state, it did not restore that which was truly endogenous. Most of the main churches today have structures and mind-sets that are sectarian. Even good church leaders are prone to confuse their own ego with the will of God, and to impose their own agenda in the guise of religion. In a Celtic style church, leaders have a Rule of Life, are accountable to a soul friend, and the wider church overseers are part of a local church community and under the authority of its leader.

How, in our multi-cultural and multi-racial society do churches reflect the indigenous principle outside native reservations? Some create ethnic churches. Ethnic church services may have their place, but that place is best as part of the local and wider church's journey. For Africans, Hispanics, White Euro Americans, and Natives are all brothers and sisters of Christ. One way to put flesh upon those relationships is through the emergence of villages of God that have unity in diversity.

As we have seen, in the early years of church in Celtic-speaking lands tribal leaders gave lands by the strategic highways of sea and river to church planters who established communities of daily prayer, education, hospitality, and land care. Peoples monastery churches served as daily prayer base, school, library, scriptorium/arts center, drop-in, library, school, health center. They had farms with livestock and crops, workshops such as wood, spinning and milling. They were open to the world. They offered soul friends, training, and even entertainment. Children, housewives, farm workers and visitors would wander in and out. Visitors brought news from overseas. They were villages of God. Each had its own flavor in worship and values (Rule) yet each was connected with the universal church through common practices, prayers, and priests ordained in the apostolic succession.

Although our society is vastly different, changing trends again require churches that are more than single-building Sunday-only congregations.

- A twenty-four-hour society calls for seven day a week churches.

- A cafe society calls for churches that are eating places.

- A traveling society calls for churches that provide accommodation and reconnect with the hostel movement.

- A stressed society calls for churches that provide spaces for retreat and meditation.

- A multi-choice society calls for churches that have a choice of styles and facilities.

- A fragmented society calls for holistic models and whole life discipling.

- An eco-threatened society calls for more locally sustainable communities.

A Financial Times article by Henry Mance during the 2020 Coronavirus pandemic heralded "the end of the office." "The office was the defining building of our times" he wrote. He quoted William Whyte who summed up the organization man as someone who had "left home, spiritually as well as physically." Mance concluded "Physically, we will now spend more time in our homes and our neighborhoods; perhaps we will return there spiritually too." This "return" to place and to neighborhood is the kairos, the timely opportunity for the Celtic Way to re-surge.[20]

A contemporary Celtic model is incarnational. Christians embody and continue Christ's life and work—they make community and build God's kingdom. As the heart is to a person so a Celtic church is to the community or network it serves.

It has a heart: for God—sustained by daily prayer; for others—sustained by hospitality and nurture; for the world—cherishing the earth and society. In many churches the focus of time and energy is maintenance of a program or building. This produces overload, so that any new leads from God are blocked out. In a Celtic-style church, programs and buildings are

20. Mance, "*Rise and fall*"

provisional; they flow out of Spirit-led initiatives, and when that tide ebbs they are beached.

A church that embraces a Celtic spirit starts its journey from where it is. It discerns which features of "a Celtic church" it can move towards on its own or with others. Some may enrich existing services with Celtic prayer patterns. Certain congregations may introduce daily prayer, a rule of life for core members and soul friends; others may re-locate from an anachronistic building to a house of prayer. A church with resources and a viable site may review which of these features of a village of God they can develop or (if their site is not a hub) link up with: Sacred, praying or worship spaces * Eating space * Accommodation space * Learning space * Art space * Wild space * Conference space * Recreation space * Godly play space * Eco space * Shop space * Work space * Meditation space * WIFI space.

Even if there are ethnic as well as multi-racial worship services, most of these spaces can be shared by all as brothers and sisters. A Celtic church is like the hub of a wheel with spokes that reach into work, social, educational, health, sport, business, and care networks. However diverse, they are marked by the ABC values of Authenticity, Blessing and Culture-friendship. Like yeast in dough, these gradually become part of a transforming sense of community.

The churches of indigenous Celtic-speaking peoples in the early Christian centuries did some distinctive things. They found ways, in a patriarchal society, for women to become inspired role models and leaders. When the doctrine of original sin caused people to separate God from the created world, they found ways of re-connecting with God within creation. When top-down constructs and organization issued from top-down churches they found ways of working with Jesus within the patterns of the people. When dualism split the psyche of the western church they continued to relate to that which is of God in every person. When the western church reduced the Trinity to a dry formulation, they sustained a love affair with the Communion of Loves in the heart of God. Ita, the spiritual foster mother of Brendan, dreamed that an angel gave her three precious jewels. These gleamed from inside her breasts. She understood that these represented the Father, the Son, and the Holy Spirit. The Trinity would dwell within her and constitute, so to speak, her love life.

When Christianity became prey to top-down churches in thrall to power politics and competition they kept alive the Jesus movement as a peoples' monastic movement where all can be brothers and sisters, following

The Way together. Such Celtic saints call us to see the Creator's imprint in every people, and to invite Jesus to reveal himself in the patterns of each people, to redeem what is displeasing to him and to forge new teamwork.

As we reflect upon Jesus's loved disciple and his loved mother at the cross, and how Jesus gives them into each other's care, and how they become the heart of a world-wide family which later was called the church, may we live that quality of family in the place where we live., may this become America's way of listening, its passion and greatness.

James Mackey points out in the Preface to *Celtic Spirituality* (Paulist Press) that a this-worldly spirituality breathes through the Bible. He writes:

> "The Divine Word, which continuously creates the world, takes human form in Jesus of Nazareth who, as life-giving spirit, forms his extended body from fellow-humans down the ages. It is to this body that the physical world itself looks for a like liberation from evil and finitude, the liberations of the sons of God, until in the eschaton all together share eternal fulfillment in the new heaven-and-earth". It is this biblical spirituality that breathes through Celtic spirituality, which has never fallen prey to the separation of the individual from the rest of life. So when I accept Jesus, I see myself as the first fruits of a new creation.[21]

Mackey points out that another significant genre in Celtic literature—the voyage—anchors the this-worldly nature of Celtic nature even more strongly. The archetypal religious imagery of the exodus and return, in which God travels towards and through creation so that creation can travel to its fulfillment in creative union with God, is illustrated through a visionary voyage through the familiar world which all the time tries to envisage a perfected but similarly structured world to come, continuous with this world.

So, in the allegorical story of Brendan's voyage they followed the advice of a Steward and for several years spent Holy Thursday on the Island of Sheep, Easter on the whale, Easter to Pentecost on the Paradise of Birds, and Christmas to Epiphany with the monks of the monastery of St. Ailbe whose food was replenished miraculously from heaven and who never grew old. That is no doubt why Irish Christians thought it was important that they were buried in their "place of resurrection". This may be quaint to us, but it held the truth that in the resurrected life they would in some way be connected with the physical world they already knew.

---

21. Davies, *Celtic Spirituality* xv

So, the message to over individualistic conservative evangelical critics is "Be born again as a first fruits of God's new creation". Open your eyes to see the divine presence flowing in to creation through Mary, the angels, the holy men and women, into the very elements themselves. Become elemental believers.

5

Brendan's Return

A New American Dream

History, despite its wrenching pain, cannot be unlived,
but if faced with courage, need not be lived again.

MAYA ANGELOU.

The Way Ahead

THE EIGHTH CENTURY *NAVIGATIO Brendani* reflects the journey motif. This archetypal motif is found in one of the world's earliest religious texts, the Babylonian epic *Gilgamesh*, and in the Hopi's tracing of their origin and destiny. It is reflected in the Buddhist Four-fold Path, and in the Chinese Dao. It is fundamental to the biblical Exodus story which is carried over into the Christian understanding of Baptism and Eucharist. It is why Roman Catholics sometimes call baptism preparation The Journey. It is doubtless why Jesus called himself The Way and why the first disciples of Jesus were known as Followers of the Way.

Brendan was a follower of The Way. He had a Rule, or Way, that honored the divine rhythms of nature, that took him across an ocean, and that discerned Jesus in a First Nation people. The Brendan myth teaches all peoples that *"Blessed are the meek: they shall inherit the earth"* (Matthew 5:5). This is the ancient yet ever-living Way that indigenous and settler, black and white can now learn to travel together.

The story of Brendan's journey to America is not just myth. In 1976 the journalist Tim Severin, convinced that the story of Brendan's seven-year voyage across the Atlantic Ocean to a new land and back had the ring of truth, built a replica of Brendan's currach using traditional tools, and succeeded in reaching North America.

It is believed that the Latin texts of *Navigatio Sancti Brendani Abbatis* (The Voyage of St. Brendan the Abbot) dating back to at least 800AD reflect the historical journey of Brendan's (c. 489–583) seven-year voyage across the Atlantic Ocean to a new land and his return. Handcrafted, using traditional tools, the 36-foot (11 m), two-masted boat was built of Irish ash and oak, hand-lashed together with nearly two miles (3 km) of leather thong, wrapped with 49 traditionally tanned ox hides, and sealed with wool grease.

Between May 1976 and June 1977, Severin and his crew sailed the Brendan 4,500 miles (7,200 km) from Ireland to Peckford Island, Newfoundland, stopping at the Hebrides and Iceland en-route. His book[1] The Brendan Voyage, became an international best seller, translated into sixteen languages.

Before that Ian Cameron researched a credible itinerary followed by Brendan or later pre-Viking Irish saints inspired by him, based on the information contained in *the Navigatio Sancti Brendani*.[2] Their motive was to be abandoned to the God who had come among them, and to discover places where that similar spirit of abandonment and oneness with the Creator could be found or kindled.

Cameron thinks they left Ireland at The Celtic Sea at Dingle, stopped at St. Kilda's in the Outer Hebrides, at the Faeroes (the name is Danish for sheep), at Vagar (the Isle of Birds), at somewhere like Madeira in the Tropic of Cancer, at San Miguel (the island with bad water) in the Azores, the Sargasso Sea (which resembled a "thick, curdled mass"), at Long Island in the Bahamas ("flat and almost level with the sea"), at the coral reefs of the Caribbean with their sailfish, swordfish, and other large fish, at Jamaica (the fragrant island of trees and fountains), at ice-bergs ("the bejeweled temples" off the Greenland glaciers), at the volcanic Jan Meyen (the black island with its column of smoke), at Iceland south of Mount Hekla (ragged, rocky slag covered with smiths forges) with its burning clinkes, lava stench and sulphur aftermath of volcanic explosions, at Newfoundland's fog belt (with its "banks of vapor"), and finally the discovery that they had landed

---

1. Severin, *Brendan Voyage.*
2. Cameron, *Lodestone and Evening Star.*

not on an island but on a continent including a river too broad to cross. We may visualize Brendan's holy crew landing somewhere not too far from Chesapeake Bay, pushing inland, crossing the Appalachians and finding their way barred by the mighty branch of the Mississippi, and being welcomed by a nearby Indian tribe.

The Vikings, writing of their eleventh century exploration of North America repeatedly state that when they reached the New World they found the Irish already there. The story of Ari Marson which is related by two Icelandic chroniclers, mentions the Irish in Baffin Island, Novia Scotia, the Skraelings (Indians), Vineland the Good (Massachusetts) and White Man's Land (Hvitramenaland) which is sometimes called Great Ireland, and where Ari, who had been baptized in Ireland, was made a chief by the inhabitants.

Seldom in the history of sea-faring have such long and liminal voyages been made in such frail and homespun craft. Seldom, also, has a story such as Brendan's become such an iconic myth.

Will Toms' vision of "The return of Brendan" is both a parable for our time and a narrative waiting to be written in the lives of a new generation who will leave behind their excess baggage, abandon themselves into the arms of Providence, and entrust themselves to those who show a welcome.

The abiding Brendan myth suggests that he understands that Jesus, the eternal Word from whom creation comes, and the supreme example of what a human being should be, was already present among the American Indian people who befriended him. Centuries later than the original Brendan the Protestant settlers in North America, unlike Brendan, made a distinction between nature and the God of the Bible. They thought of nature as part of the demonic world that needed to be conquered, as a community of objects rather than as a community of subjects.

Three factors which make "the return of Brendan" more than a fantasy are 1) the "save the environment" movement 2) post-colonial theology 3) the growth of new monasticism.

The Save the Environment Movement

In her ground-breaking best seller *This Changes Everything* (Penguin 2015) Naomi Klein concludes that "the systems that dominate our economics, politics and much religion are based on humankind taking more and more from a finite world. The climate crisis reveals that earth is fighting back." Her book illustrates the truth expressed by Columbanus: If you trample the earth the earth will trample you. Critics argue that the USA constitution epitomized the fulfillment of this anthropocentric view of the universe and of the bible. The US passion for "the rights of Man" omitted "the rights of nature". God may be using the climate crisis to turn blind biblicists into new Brendans.

Klein lays bare how the heart of our economic model is grow or die. In the 1980s President Reagan's Interior Secretary James Watt likened environmentalists' campaigning for organized regulation to improve the environment to the Nazi subordination of persons to the state. Free world trade has vastly increased exports and imports of fossil fuel-enabled products—much based on greed, none of it based on care for the environment. This is now in conflict with the imperative of the environment crisis: steward or die. We have to come out of denial. A worldview needs to arise that sees nature, other nations and our own neighbors as partners in a grand project of mutual reinvention.

Klein gives examples of how we filter new information in ways that protect our preferred world view and repel unwelcome information such as the Heartland Conferences hosted by money-making climate change deniers. Greed is presented as a good: ever increasing neo-colonial plunder of the world's resources engines the market. Climate change requires us to admit that we need to plan our societies to reflect our goals and values, not leave them to "the magic of the market". The trillionaires pay nothing for treating the globe as a free waste dump.

The World Trade Organisation opposes as "protectionist" local efforts to improve their countries, yet the Stern Review on The Economics of Climate Change described the $1 trillion subsidies to global fossil fuel companies as "the greatest market failure the world has ever seen." The global producers got patents for their products; they distributed them world-wide, spewing out vast carbon emissions. A de-stabilized climate, Klein points out, is the cost of a deregulated global capitalism.

In 1988 Time Magazine made the Earth the "Person of the Year". Journalist Thomas Sancton wrote "In many pagan societies the earth was seen as a mother, a fertile giver of life . . . The Judeo-Christian tradition introduced a radically different concept . . ."—that a monotheist God invited humans to dominate it—which could be interpreted as an invitation to use nature as a convenience. This is in fact a travesty of the concept that lies at the heart of the Bible, that all creation flows from the heart of Christ (John 1:1–4). John

Muir, an early US pioneer of the environmental movement, who helped found the Sierra Club in 1892, excoriated the industrialists who dammed wild rivers etc. To him they were heathens, "devotees of ravaging commercialism" who "instead of raising their eyes to the God of the mountains, lift them to the Almighty Dollar."[3]

Endless extraction ruins the planet. To deal with this requires us to face that we are vulnerable and inter-connected. These are religious fundamentals. It means admitting that the power relationship between humans and the earth is different to what we have assumed for centuries. Even the famous economist Keynes advocated a transition to a post-growth society.

Indigenous peoples are using their recognized laws to prevent e.g. pipelines and tankers ruining their lands and the planet. Enbridge Northern Gateway (a First Nations Coalition opposing this pipeline) has unified British Columbia. Many non-Natives are beginning to see that the Indigenous ways have much to teach us. Missisauga Nishnaabeg educator Leanne Simpson described First Nations governmental systems as "designed to promote more life". She describes the extractivist mind-set as "stealing" and indigenous cultures as "continuous rebirth". We need people in Government with the Brendan spirit. Canada is ahead of the USA in this area. The British Columbia Truth and Reconciliation Commission on De-Colonisation has made huge progress. The BC Ministry of Education has made Indigenous Studies a compulsory part of every school curriculum.

Klein concludes that the climate crisis calls for a new world view. That is why new Brendans, for whom salvation includes the restoration of Eden, are needed as never before.

The Growth of Postcolonial Theology

A second factor is that accompanying the increasing recognition by former colonial powers of their mistreatment of indigenous peoples and blindness towards their spiritualities is the rise among churches of post-colonial theology for which Brendan's return is a metaphor.

This emerged in the 1990s as a recognition that the winners write the history and interpret the sacred texts in the light of their inherited presuppositions. The colonizers had to try and put themselves into the mind-set of indigenous peoples, whether in Africa, Australasia or America, and interpret biblical texts in the light of their new recognition of inherited

3. Muir, "Who Was John Muir?".184

pre-suppositions. In postcolonial theology, students compare and contrast and learn from one another. Just as they interpret the Old Testament in the light of the Defenseless Love of Jesus, the Eternal Lamb of God, so they interpret the whole Bible through the lens of the people among whom they are guests. R.S. Sugirtharajah argues that postcolonial theology is held back by Western reluctance to analyse the theological implications of colonial imperialism.[4] However, theologians from the colonized non-West such as C. S. Song and Chung Hyun Kyung have long been theologizing with reflection or even resistance against the colonizing West.

Canada's Mennonite Church has taken a lead in pioneering fresh theology in partnership with indigenous believers. Canada's Truth and Reconciliation Commission has summoned all churches and faith groups "in collaboration with Indigenous spiritual leaders, survivors, schools of theology, seminaries, and other religious training centers, to develop and teach curricula for all student clergy, and all clergy and staff who work in Aboriginal communities, on the need to respect Indigenous spirituality in its own right . . ."[5] Intotemak, the Indigenous Relations magazine of the Mennonite Church has published Quest for Respect, which explores questions such as How does spiritual abuse continue today? How might we repair the damage done? And what does genuine respect really look like?[6]

Only recently have western Christians studied pre-verbal scriptures of the cosmos, recognized that science reveals the principles of co-operation, flow and energy in the cosmos, and developed truly biblical ways of seeing. These help us recover the manifestation of the divine in the natural world. Thomas Berry[7] describes the period before verbal scriptures as "the period of unarticulated but deeply felt response to the scripture of the cosmos". He categorizes the geo-biological periods as Paleozoic (600–220 million years ago), Mesozoic (220–65 million years), Cenozoic (the last 65 million years), and now the new Eco-zoic age. Understanding of the Eco-zoic age was facilitated by space travel. Astronaut Ed Mitchell, when he viewed earth from space, said ". . . suddenly there was a non-rational way of understanding—there was a purpose of flow, of energy, of time, of space in the cosmos". Only recently have western Christians begun to understand that a degraded world leads to a degraded inner world. Rachel Carson's Silent

---

4. Sugirtharajah, Bible.

5. Converging Pathways Call to Action #60.

6. Friesen, and Heinrichs, Quest for Respect.

7. Berry, Sacred Universe.

Spring published in 1962 inspired a radical new generation of environmentalists. In 1972 The Club of Rome published The Limits to Growth.

In his book[8] Kent Nerburn points out that although the customs and languages of the native tribes differed, they shared a common belief that the earth is a spiritual presence that must be honored, not mastered. "Unfortunately, western Europeans who came to these shores, unlike Brendan, had a contrary belief. To them, the entire American continent was a beautiful but savage land that it was their right and their duty to tame and use as they saw fit. As we enter the twenty-first century, Western civilization is confronting the inevitable results of this Euro-American philosophy of dominance. We have gotten out of balance within our earth, and the very future of our planet depends on our capacity to restore the balance."

This re-alignment is not a matter of Right versus Left. Globalism and mass migration make many feel they have been overlooked. In her novel[9] Barbara Kingsolver charts what she sees as the breakdown of American society. Indeed, the old world order is changing. One billion new workers have joined the labor market. Seismic changes bring insecurity. People feel their communities are changing but they have not been consulted. They seek to anchor themselves in a sense of place, belonging, and identity. Social media inflame prejudices. Is there a way of being present to a place without getting stuck or vindictive? If followers of the Way do not give a lead, and capture the people's imagination with integrity, we lose the battle. The new Brendans value the sacredness of place but do not get stuck in it for they never cease to journey.

The Growth of New Monasticism

In a letter to his brother Karl-Friedrick on the 14th of January, 1935 Dietrich Bonhoeffer wrote ". . . the restoration of the church will surely come only from a new type of monasticism which has nothing in common with the old but a complete lack of compromise in a life lived in accordance with the Sermon on the Mount in the discipleship of Christ. I think it is time to gather people together to do this."[10] The writer Phyllis Tickle spoke much of "The Great Emergence". As traditional forms of Christianity decline she

8. Nerburn, *Wisdom.*
9. Kingsolver, *Unsheltered.*
10. Kelly and Burton, *Testament,* 424.

envisaged thousands of little experiments, which might loosely be called a new monastic movement, shooting up in unlikely places.

However, new monasticism calls us to jettison all forms of empire building and to start at Ground Zero, and who wants that? New monasticism prays for a re-indigenisation of our way of being, for Jesus is indigenous to the cosmos, the creation, and common humanity. Jesus is hidden in new monasticism: like a root out of dry ground, there is nothing that we should desire him (Isaiah 53:2).

In 2004 a Christian community at Rutba House, Durham called together a group of Anabaptists, Catholics, Mainline Protestants, and Evangelicals to discuss ways in which their lives could be understood and deepened as a neo-monastic movement. Their statement includes "Twelve Marks of a New Monasticism" which they hope will help to facilitate conversation about this movement of the Spirit. The Twelve Marks are:

1. Relocation to Abandoned Places of Empire
2. Sharing Economic Resources with Fellow Community Members and the Needy Among Us
3. Hospitality to the Stranger
4. Lament for Racial Divisions and Active Pursuit of a Just Reconciliation
5. Humble Submission to Christ's Body, The Church
6. Intentional Formation and a Community Rule
7. Nurturing Common Life Amongst Members of Intentional Community
8. Support for Celibates, Married Couples and Children
9. Geographical Proximity to Community Members
10. Care for the Plot of God's Earth Given to Us and Supporting Our Local Economies
11. Peacemaking in the Midst of Violence and Conflict Resolution
12. Commitment to a Disciplined Contemplative Life.[11]

New monasticism requires that we root out prejudice and cease to judge people. Yet according to Hugo Mercier and Dan Sperber,[12] we are hard-wired to resist facts that challenge our existing beliefs. We are all slaves

---

11. Simpson, *High Street Monasteries.*
12. Mercier and Sperber, *Enigma.*

to our "partisan brain". According to statistics from the Implicit Association Test (IAT) based at Harvard University, very few of us are totally without prejudice. In order to discover what we might be hiding, researchers at Harvard devised a form of questionnaire that measures the associations we make between "good" and "bad", "black" and "white", "gay" and "straight", and so on.[13] We are good at masking our true feelings and may not even be aware what they are.

Jesus commands us *"Do not judge"* (Matthew 7:1). New monasticism calls us to a life-long practice of stripping off the false ego with its prejudice and judging. This does not mean that we have no convictions. It is as much a challenge to Christians as it is to others. Protestantism has been described as a list of opinions: every time someone forms a new opinion they start a new church. But Catholics and Orthodox can be no less opiniated.

Traditional monasticism starts with the three vows of poverty, chastity, and obedience. New monasticism translates these applications into universal, life-giving principles: simplicity, purity, and obedience.

My book[14] *New Celtic Monasticism for Everyday People* gives the story of the international Community of Aidan and Hilda. Simon Reed's[15] *Followers of the Way* unpacks its way of life. It was launched almost simultaneously in UK and US. The Irish singer Paul Kyle sang "O Ireland" and other songs at the launch. He then set up a US ministry called Brendan's Brunch. In 2017 he released his *The Voyage of the Bright Hostage*. The first song is *St. Brendan's Company*. This album introduces you to the "wild goose" (the term the Celtic Saints used for the Spirit of God) and shows how He/She is involved in the whole of our lives.

The community of Aidan and Hilda describes itself as "a world-wide people who journey with God, reconnecting with the Spirit and the Scriptures, the saints and the streets, the seasons and soil". Its first three priorities are the adoption of three Great Beatitudes of Jesus:

a) Simplicity, that we may experience more of God's generosity. Simplicity strips us of possessiveness and is rooted in Jesus's words *"Blest are the poor in spirit."* (Matthew 5:3).

Simplicity means the willingness to be poor or rich for God according to God's direction. We resist the temptations to be greedy or possessive,

---

13. Project Implicit *Harvard Implicit Bias Test*
14. Simpson, *New Celtic Monasticism.*
15. Reed, *Followers of the Way.*

and we will not manipulate people or creation for our own ends. The Community of Aidan and Hilda Way of Life.

> We original Americans have generally been despised by our white conquerors for our poverty and simplicity. They forget, perhaps, that our religion forbade the accumulation of wealth and the enjoyment of luxury. To us, as to other spiritually-minded people in every age and race, the love of possessions is a snare, and the burdens of a complex society a source of needless peril and temptation . . . It was the rule of our life to share the fruits of our skill and success with our less fortunate brothers and sisters. Thus, we kept our spirit free from the clog of pride, avarice, or envy, and carried out, as we believed, the divine decree—a matter profoundly important to us . . . This lust for money, power and conquest did not escape moral condemnation at our hands, nor did we fail to contrast this conspicuous trait with the spirit of the meek and lowly Jesus . . . Ohijesa[16]

b) Purity of motive, that we may experience more of God's love. Purity strips us of idols and is rooted in Jesus's words *"Blest are the pure in heart, for they shall see God."* Matthew 5:8.

"We respect every person as belonging to God, and we are available to them with generosity and openness." The Community of Aidan and Hilda Way of Life.

"We have always believed that love is good but lust destroys . . ." Ohijesa

c) Obedience to God in each person, that we may experience more of God's freedom.

"We listen attentively to that which is of God in each person" Community of Aidan and Hilda

Obedience strips us of both mistreating and subservience to others and is rooted in Jesus's words *"Blest are the meek, for they shall inherit the earth"* (Matthew 5:5).

"It appears that (white people) are anxious to pass on their religion to all other races but keep very little of it themselves. I have not yet seen the meek inherit the earth, or the peace-makers receive high honor." Ohijesa

"Indian faith sought the harmony of man with his surroundings; the other sought the dominance of surroundings." Chief Luther Standing Bear

"Sell a country! Why not sell the air, the great sea as well as the earth?" Tecumseh, Shawnee

---

16. Murray, *A Wasicu (White Man)*

Chief Too-hool-hopol-suit said to General Howard in Washington in 1878, after he ordered his people to re-locate to a reservation: "Who are you that you should ask us to talk and then tell me I shan't talk? Are you the Great Spirit? Did you make the world?"

Simplicity strips us of empire building. Purity strips us of prejudice. Obedience strips us of racism. The fruit of these three Life-giving Principles is love. They lead us to dwell in the Three Loves in God's heart as we journey through life.

Will Toms writes: "That is the TRINITY, or as I tend to think the FOUR: Father, Holy Spirit, Son, and Bride. And the Bride, I think, may in some way include all of Creation, from which we were formed, and for which we've been tasked with Stewardship and/or possibly Headship of. As Christ is our Head, we are its head, within Him. And ultimately we are all ONE in the Father, to Whom we've been reconciled, the Shema."

Waymarks

CAH suggests that as we journey on the Way in the spirit of Brendan, The Creator gives us Waymarks or way-finders. Here are ten waymarks:

Life-Long Learning through Head, Heart and Hands

"Make all tribes my learners (disciples) Jesus" (Matthew 28:19.).

"Knowledge was inherent in all things. The world was a library . . ." Chief Luther Standing Bear.

Celtic followers of Jesus believed in two books, the Bible and Nature. We "new Brendans" seek to learn something from each book every day of our lives. We also learn from elders and inspiring people, and from life, by reflecting back on what we have learned each day before we sleep. Some call this ancient practice the Examen.

Great Provider, I leave behind my anger and arrogance, my urge to control and my nontransparent ways; I throw overboard possessiveness, self-righteousness, and demonization of the other.

Journey Through Life

The Irish missionary monk Columbanus advised us to think of ourselves as guests of the earth, and as perpetual pilgrims from our birth to our death. The journey motif is central to ancient religious myths and to the biblical stories. It dominates the ancient Babylonian story of Gilgamesh, the Homeric epics, the Hebrew Exodus, the wanderings of Buddha, and the Hopi people's tracing of their origins.

"You have made me cross the good road, and the road of difficulties, and where they cross, the place is holy. Day in, day out, for evermore, You are the life of things." Black Elk, Oglala Sioux.

Some voyagers heed this prayer of Polynesian Archbishop Winston Halapua:

> O Jesus, be the canoe that holds me in the sea of life,
> Be the steer that keeps me straight,
> Be the outrigger that supports me in time of great temptation.
> Let your Spirit be my sail that carries me through each day
> As I journey steadfastly on the long voyage of life.

We journey with a soul friend or elder, one who seeks to discern with us where we are on the journey, what the Spirit is doing in our lives, and what next steps we should take. A soul friend is like gentle rain on dry seedlings, an anchor to a blown ship, a window onto a new world, a loving presence when we feel bereft.

As we journey sometimes retreat to spend time alone with God, and we go on pilgrimages.

Keeping Rhythms of Prayer, Work and Re-Creation

New Brendans pause to pray in the rhythm of the sun's rising, zenith and setting:

> We arise today in the radiance of sun . . .
> As the sun rides high at noon, may the Sun of Righteousness shine
> upon us . . .
> As the sun settles in the west, in you may we find our rest.

"Our whole life is prayer because every act of our life is, in a very real sense, a religious act . . . Our daily devotions are more important to us than food . . . We wake at daybreak and step down to the water's edge. Here we throw handfuls of water into our face, or plunge in bodily . . . Whenever in the course of the day, we come upon a scene that is strikingly beautiful—we pause for a moment in the attitude of worship". Ohijesa

New voyagers restore a rhythm like that of Moses' people. Every week the community entered into an exercise in trust together; they gave in to their need for rest, believing that if they did this God would care for their needs. Every week the community used the space created by not working to turn itself to God. Through this concrete discipline they lived out their conviction that the work they accomplished in six days would be enough and God could be trusted with running the world while they rested. This daily and weekly rhythm was their earliest pattern for their life together in God's presence. Christians who buy into a culture of busyness, hurry, and overload miss the rhythms and ruin relationships.

Wholesome and Hospitable Life-Style

We do not live as consumers but we celebrate the simple things of life that God gives to us. We do not complicate life—we arrange our homes and schedules to reflect the God-given features of our personalities and place. We practice hospitality of the heart and home.

We Cherish and Are Cherished by Creation

"We look upon creation as a sacrament, reflecting the glory of God, and seek to meet God through his creation, to bless it and celebrate it . . . .We are committed to seeing it cared for and restored. We aim to be ecologically aware, to pray for God's creation, and to stand against all that would seek to violate it." The Community of Aidan and Hilda Way of Life.[17]

"Nature will be Nature still, while palaces shall decay and fall in ruins." Ojibwe

"All things are connected. Whatever befalls the earth befalls the children of earth." Chief Seattle.

The Community of Aidan and Hilda draws from American native as well as from Celtic spirituality in its marking of the seasons, as in this mid-summer ceremony of earth blessing:

How precious is the soil that God has made.

17. The Community of Aidan and Hilda Way of Life

A single seed planted in it will bring forth a hundred seeds.
How beautiful is the soil that God has made.
Frail seeds blown by gentle winds become garlands
of color flowering in crevice and cranny.
How mysterious is the soil that God has made . . .
How hospitable is the soil that God has made . . .
How like a mother is the soil that God has made.
It contains us and feeds us, it warms us and holds us.[18]
From *Celtic Prayer Book Volume 3: Healing the Land* (Kevin Mayhew)

Overcoming Evils in Ourselves and in Our Communities

Many of Brendan's compatriots were inspired by the fathers and mothers of the Egyptian deserts, who ceaselessly waged war against eight deadly sins that we would call expressions of the false ego. These included greed, lust, envy, despondency, anger, boredom, love of flattery, and pride. The destructive passions rob us of the freedom to make real choices and act on them. The fear of abandonment and the compulsive need for approval that many of us have carried over from childhood also rob us of our freedom to choose the way of love.

The new Brendans make time to do the inner work on our false ego and its deceitful manifestations. Those in charge who engage in this work do not fit others into frame-works and pre-suppositions of their own false ego. Rather, they seek to draw out what is of God in each person who is treated as of equal worth.

When Muslims do this inner work (the greater Jihad) they do away with the need for military Jihad.

Each day we pray and live so that God's ways come on earth as in heaven.

Healing What Is Broken

"We renounce the spirit of self-sufficient autonomy and commit to a more holistic approach . . . We not only lay hands on the sick and pray for their healing, we also "lay hands" on every part of God's world to bless it and recognize its right to wholeness . . . We work with people of good will so that our lands may be led by God and

18. Simpson, *Liturgies from Lindisfarne*, 290

become healed lands . . ." The Community of Aidan and Hilda Way of Life.

"I have asked some of the great white chiefs where they get their authority to say to the Indian that he shall stay in one place, while he sees white men going where they please. They cannot tell me . . . When the white man treats an Indian as they treat each other, then we will have no more wars. We shall all be alike—brothers of one father and one mother, with one sky above us and one government for all. Then the Great Spirit Chief who rules above will smile upon this land, and send rain to wash out the bloody spots made by brothers' hands from the face of the earth. I hope that no more groans of wounded men and women will ever go to the ear of the Great Spirit Chief above, and that all people may be one people". Chief Joseph

The new voyagers are humble and they heal. When tribes were forced out of their homes and had to walk to a strange place their route was called a Trail of Tears. I met a white believer who knew that "when we act out of our wounds we are not nice". He researched the original trail and walked it alone as an act of contrition and healing. Others have re-traced the routes of the papal crusades whereby Christians re-captured Jerusalem by military force, killing innocent civilians along the way. Descendants of victims welcomed them with tears of forgiveness.

Listening Out of Stillness

"Learning to listen to God is a skill that has almost been lost, and which takes many years to acquire. We seek to cultivate an interior silence that recognizes and sets aside discordant voices, to respond to unexpected or disturbing promptings of God, to widen our horizons, to develop "the eye of the eagle" and see and hear God through his creation." The Community of Aidan and Hilda Way of Life.

Silence was meaningful to the Lakota, as to many tribes. It was regardful of the rule that "thought comes before speech".

"The silent man was ever to be trusted, while the man ever ready with speech was never taken seriously." Chief Luther Standing Bear (Sioux)

"There is no quiet place in the white man's cities, no place to hear the leaves of spring or the rustle of insect's wings. Perhaps it is because I am a savage and do not understand, but the clatter only seems to insult the ears." Chief Seattle

"Our young people, raised under the old rules of courtesy, never indulged in the present habit of talking incessantly and all at the same time. To do so would not only have been impolite but foolish; for poise, so much admired as a social grace, could not be accompanied by restlessness . . . We believe profoundly in silence—the sign of a perfect equilibrium. Silence is the absolute poise or balance of body, mind, and spirit . . . If you ask us, "What is silence?" we will answer, "It is the Great Mystery. The holy silence is God's Voice". If you ask, "What are the fruits of silence?", we will answer . . . "Silence is the cornerstone of character." Ohijesa (Sioux)

> "Listening is a skill that has almost been lost, and which takes many years to acquire. At the age of thirteen I became a Christian. Three years later I nearly became an atheist. Why? The people I read about in the Bible listened to God: the Christians I knew did not. The Christians I knew merely told people "All you need is Jesus" failing to take into account that Jesus said "You have ears—why don't you listen?" Then I met some Christians who did listen. They used to say "God gave us two ears and one mouth—why don't we listen twice as much as we talk?" That set me on a life-long quest to discover the art of listening. I found that this faculty has become a victim of endless sound-bites that don't come from God, and of capitalism's "hidden persuaders" who misinform our unconscious thinking in order to sell their products. The Bible story of Samuel, however, gave me hope. For he, also, grew up in a society in which listening was a lost art." From Waymarks for the Journey entry for August 13 published by Kevin Mayhew.

Building Community

"We seek to cultivate solidarity with all people in everything except sin . . . to weave together again . . . the God-given strands of Christianity which later became separated." The Community of Aidan and Hilda Way of Life.

"We do not want churches because they will teach us to quarrel about God . . . We may quarrel with men sometimes about things on this earth. But we never quarrel about God. We do not want to learn that." Chief Joseph, Nez Perce.

This Way challenges us to ask How do we go with the grain of the human communities among whom we work?; how do we heal what is broken in our communities?; how do we make community with all other parts of the Body of Christ throughout the world?

Justice

"Our mission also includes speaking out for the poor, the powerless, and those unjustly treated." The Community of Aidan and Hilda Way of Life

"Do you call yourselves Christians? Does then the religion of Him whom you call your Savior inspire your spirit, and guide your practices? Surely not. It is recorded of him that a bruised reed he never broke . . ." Joseph Brant (Thayendanegea), Mohawk.[19]

"I have learned that one great principle (of the whites' religion) is "do to others as you wish them to do to you". . . The settlers on our lands never seem to think of it, if we are to judge by their actions." Black Hawk, Sauk.

Voyagers vow to love the poor, stand for justice, and care for the bruised reed. New voyagers often make this promise:

I vow to

1. Learn something each day, from inspired Scriptures, people or nature.

2. Voyage each day with the Great Spirit, with stops for soul friending, retreat or pilgrimage.

3. Pray in the daily rhythms of the sun, morning, noon and night, work in the seasons of the body, create in the seasons of the soul.

4. Overcome some bad thing, in me or in the human community.

5. Live simply, without clutter in my belongings and thoughts.

6. Cherish something in creation and let the Creator speak to me through creation.

7. Heal a wound in myself, someone else or our wider community.

8. Listen to the Great Spirit, store Wisdom and share it.

9. Unite my heart to my neighbors, my people, and those Jesus calls his "other flocks".

10. Reach out to love each person, share good news of Jesus and build just ways in the world.

19. Friesen, and Heinrichs, *Quest for Respect.*

As they become steeped in this ancient yet new Way, voyagers develop "the eye of the eagle". They see through what is sham in national and church personas, but also see the imprints of the Creator, and they know that transformation is possible.

Healing the Land

Those who follow this Way of Life commit to the healing of wounded group memory. Jack Stapleton, the first US Guardian of CAH wrote the following, extracted from a series of articles in its magazine *The Wild Goose:*

> There is no doubt that our land, America, needs healing . . . Holy Scripture makes no separation between the people and the land. The woundedness of the people causes the land to bleed. The woundedness of the land, caused by the abuse or neglect of its people, exacerbates the woundedness of the people.
>
> What if the Celtic way of Christianity had survived? Certainly the Christian history of the West would make dramatically different reading. Perhaps doctrinal differences between Christians would not have been set in the reinforced concrete of denomination institutions. Perhaps we might have been spared the fragmentation of Christian life into inadequate enclaves of sacramentalism, evangelicalism, charismatic renewal, and social proclamation. Perhaps Christians might never have been drawn into an unholy conspiracy to justify the rape of the earth. Perhaps men and women in Christ would never have been confined in deadly stereotypes of ministry and authority . . .
>
> What if there were a people group whose values and pattern of life were similar to the Celtic peoples in the time when Christianity first reached them? What if these people lived in the heart of Western civilization, but were relatively untouched by the Gospel? What if these people could be given the Gospel through one of their own and develop their own, peculiar form of contemporary Christianity that might serve as a model for those of us of European descent looking for a new model for being the Body of Christ?
>
> The native peoples of North America, the people group we call Indians, have never been completely assimilated into the Eurocentric culture of Western civilization. It is true that the Indian peoples have been touched by the Gospel. In light of the history of evangelism in North America, it might be more aptly put that they were not so much touched as bludgeoned by the Gospel. Even

the best of the Western missionaries still communicated a Gospel locked in the baggage of European civilization.

I am not speaking of the sin of conquest and physical warfare at this point. All peoples are stained with that sin and no nation can claim innocence. However, one sin committed against the native Americans which could be seen as an area for the healing of the land was committed not by the soldiers, but by the missionaries. In presenting the Gospel to the native peoples of America, our ancestors warned them that to embrace the Gospel meant to reject all elements of their native religion. The Gospel had to be received in European clothing or it could not be received at all.

I have made contact with the Native American Chapter of the International Reconciliation Coalition. Despite its name, this ministry is a ministry of European-Americans with several Native Americans as advisors. They do not presume to show Native Americans anything about the Christian life save for one thing: the Christian practice of confession, reconciliation and restoration. They work with Indian pastors and elders of Indian churches. Their work of repentance includes meeting with Indian leaders at sites of battles and massacres and repenting for the destruction heaped on the Native peoples and the history of broken promises that litter our past relationships. One other aspect of their work is identifying those circumstances when the Gospel was presented in ways that denied the redemptive purposes of God imbedded in the pre-conquest spirituality of the Native peoples. John Dawson, founder of the International Reconciliation Coalition,[20] speaks of God planting a redemptive purpose in the heart of every aboriginal people. When the Gospel enters a peoples' life, this redemptive purpose can be realized. One might say the redemptive purpose of the Celts was a form of Christian life both balanced and all-embracing. Native Americans may well have a similar redemptive purpose. The people who lead this ministry understand that Indian church leaders must be set free from the constraints of a culture-laden Christianity in order to recover this purpose.

The process of the healing of the land would involve three steps. First, the Church must repent of its smothering of the Gospel in the cultural trappings of Europe. Secondly, we must admit to the native American peoples that we were wrong to deny them the opportunity to "baptize" their ancient religion in the light of the Good News of Jesus. Third, we must humbly ask them to go back and do the very thing we denied them while we stand aside.

20. Dawson, *Healing America's Wounds.*

It may seem idealistic, and from the point of view of Christian orthodoxy, very risky. However, it is already going on, not, I am ashamed to say, in the mainline churches. All too often the spiritual relativism of modern mainline churches prefers to embrace an unconverted native American spirituality rather than follow the Celtic combination of an unwavering proclamation of the Gospel and the appreciation of a peoples' spiritual heritage. This process of healing is being carried out by evangelicals, pentecostals, and fundamentalists, those sectors of the Christian community so often despised by the mainstream of our culture. Already white Christian leaders are meeting with their native American counterparts, confessing their sins, seeking reconciliation and restoration. We have recently seen an example of this activity in the Southern Baptist Convention's recent apology to the African American community for their role in the sins of slavery and racism. Plans underway by various evangelical groups include pilgrimages of repentance, retracing the old slave routes from Africa to America, the path of the crusaders to Jerusalem and other similar journeys.

If these leaders are set free by our repentance and acknowledgment that we tried to foist the Gospel in an alien form, then the stage is set for the birth of a new, native Christianity in North America, one from which we may learn to live the Gospel as the Celtic saints lived it.

The Celtic knot, that beautiful interweaving design that speaks of the interconnectedness of all creation, represents a view of reality that must be recaptured. Our sins, both individual and corporate, cause the woven cord of God's created order to unravel. Celtic Christian spirituality is, with God's grace, a way to live in the balance and harmony that was God's original intent. However, much that has been done to the earth and its inhabitants must be undone before the Celtic way can be more than just faint individual attempts to swim against the stream.

Heather Johnston, a Community of Aidan and Hilda member in Australia, felt that some repentance for the historical (and current) sins of the church in relation to Aboriginal peoples was needed. So she organized an artwork (a mural with 4 panels) to be installed in Wunya Park (this is original Aboriginal land now "owned" by a church in Buderim). Three of the local Indigenous creation stories have weeping women in them. This seemed a suitable theme, and three Indigenous women artists made the installation called River of Tears for the Dispossessed. It is an expression of grief for the local sins of the church against women, children, indigenous people,

South Sea Islanders, and the environment. The five figures are the spirits of the five streams created by weeping women in the local creation legends and also Jesus's foremothers Tamar, Rahab, Bathsheba, Ruth, and Mary (as per the Matthew 1 genealogy)—iconic weeping women. The unveiling was accompanied by a talk on Jesus's Disreputable Foremothers, and they remembered women victims of the patriarchy in the church on All Souls day.

They understand that restoration is not just a biblical principle, it is possible in our time. That is why they sing:

> Rejoice rejoice, for the healing of the land
> We shout, we sing, we dance, we clap our hands.
> We went out weeping carrying the seeds
> And returned with the fruit and with shouts of joy
>
> Come like a fire, come like a cyclone,
> Holy Spirit come like a dove.
> Come in the silence, come as the comforter,
> Come to this land with your love
>
> Come as a stranger, come as a reject,
> Jesus redeemer come.
> Come like a lover, come like a mother.
> God our creator come.

Heather explains that across Australia's Uniting Church they observe a Day of Mourning on the Sunday before Australia Day to lament the ongoing effects of the invasion and colonization of Australia's First Peoples. "The Day of Mourning is an observance that was endorsed at the fifteenth Assembly in 2018 at the request of our sisters and brothers in the Uniting Aboriginal and Islander Christian Congress (UAICC). It was wonderful to see so many Uniting Church congregations take part in January 2019. The Day of Mourning worship service encourages us to pause to remember the violence and dispossession inflicted on our First Peoples, and to lament that as a Church and as Second Peoples, we were and remain complicit. It is an opportunity for us to listen and learn of the hurt that has been passed down through generations of First Peoples and the ongoing disadvantage and injustice they still experience. Importantly it is an invitation to us to follow in Christ's way of justice, healing and reconciliation, building relationships of truth and healing in our own communities and in our nation."

The Way Is Primal

In China, Tao or Dao signifies the intuitive knowing of "life" that can be grasped only by living experience. It is holistic. It is the practice of the natural order of Nature and its universal awakening. Well-being lies in aligning ourselves with this ultimate Reality. The monotheist religions—Judaism, Christianity, and Islam—can trace the DNA of this universal Way back to the Garden of Eden, when the first man and woman walked with God without any cover up. There is an imprint of Adam and Eve in all peoples.

This linking of The Way of Jesus with the Way imprinted into the very structure of the universe not only links up with the Chinese concept of Dao, it links with the Way of Perennial Wisdom. The Book of Wisdom declares: "*Wisdom knows your works and was with you when you made the world . . . For she knows and understands all things and will guide us wisely in our actions*". (Wisdom 9:7,11). The link between the Way and indigenous truths is made in the New Testament. The apostle Paul told Felix, the Tribune, when some fellow Jews criticized him for following Jesus that "*according to the Way, which they call a sect, I worship the God of our ancestors, believing everything laid down by the law or written in the prophets*" (Acts 24:14).

It also links with intimations of great minds. Father Alexander Men, in his book[21] quotes many philosophers and scientists who discern common structures, laws or patterns. He quotes James Jeans: ". . . physicists almost without exception declare that the current of knowledge does not flow via a mechanistic understanding of reality. The universe is coming to be depicted rather as a Great mind . . ." William James states: "The world will come to an end, as science assures us—it will burn or freeze up; but if the world is a constituent part of a higher harmonious pattern, then the design of the universe will not perish, surely it will bear fruit in another world." Max Planck, the originator of the quantum physics theory, concludes that the many-sided phenomena of the natural world . . ." allows the existence of a formula which, because of the purpose in things suggests a guiding reality. This all-embracing purpose presents as rational world order, to which nature and humanity are subject". A person who is in line with The Way becomes an active force in the ongoing creation of the world.

So, for us to follow The Way requires us both to yield our hearts and actions to the teachings of Jesus and also to align ourselves with the prints of the Cosmic Christ in the patterns of life.

---

21. Men, *Wellsprings of Religion*

"Why, we have followed this law you speak of for untold ages! We owned nothing, because everything is from the Creator. Food was free, land as free as sunshine and rain. Who has changed all this? The white man. And yet he says he is a believer in God! He does not seem to inherit any of the traits of his Father, nor does he follow the example set by his brother Christ." An old warrior at a meeting of young men from Sioux, Cheyenne, Cree, Ojibwe, and other tribes.

Another said: "I have come to the conclusion that this Jesus was an Indian. He was opposed to material acquisition and great possessions . . . These are not the principles upon which the white man has founded his civilization."[22]

If Jesus's first disciples were known as followers of the Way but later generations of Christians were not, what does that tell us? Does it tell us that Christians moved from being people who possessed nothing of this world into people who possessed much? That Christians ceased to be people of the Beatitudes and became prisoners of their false ego's constructs.

Research suggests that in our younger years we are dealing with the complex manifestations of our false ego, but that as people mature a higher percentage of us begin to operate from a place of empathy within our true self. It can be like that with nations. USA is no longer a young nation. The time to transition into maturity has come. "Why should you take by force from us that which you can obtain by love? Why should you destroy us who have provided you with food?" King Wahunsonacook, Powhatan.

Psychiatrist Robert Coles conducted conversations with Christian, Jewish, Muslim, and Native children for his book *The Spiritual Life of Children.*[23] A self-effacing ten-year-old Hopi girl told him "When (the land) is quiet, really quiet here, we'll all be with God—the Navajos and us and the Anglos. The land will be with God, and not with us . . . Our people are here to wait until the time comes that no one hurts the land; then we will be told that we've done our job, and we can leave". Coles described her as "a girl whose heart beats to Hopi rhythms and whose soul lay open to an entire landscape."

Antonio Gramsci said "The challenge of modernity is to live without illusions without becoming disillusioned". Those who seek to move beyond mere existence to the essence of life will find it. This is the Way of Jesus. It

22. Nerburn, *Wisdom*, 129–30

23. Coles, *Spiritual Life of Children.*

is the way of listening. It is the way of reality—those who seek reality, the truth of things, will find it.

The "return of Brendan" is beginning through new monastic grass-roots movements: "We allow God to take us where the Spirit wills, whether by gentle breeze or wild wind. The Celtic Christians had such faith in the leading of the Spirit that they gladly put to sea in small coracles and went where the wind took them. We desire this kind of openness to the leading of the Spirit" say those who take vows with the Community of Aidan and Hilda www.aidanandhilda.us[24]

We would be wise not to overlook what happened to Brendan following his return to his home country. He sought advice from his soul friend, Ita, who became known as "the foster mother of the saints of Ireland". He formed many in a monastic way of life. It was said that he gathered over three thousand brothers in the community at Clonfert, on the site of the present Church of Ireland cathedral. He went to great lengths to ensure that he was buried there, because it was his "place of resurrection". Not for the Irish this airy-fairy separation of this life from the new heaven, or of this earth from the new earth. To find one's vocation in Christ required a person to be present to the place to which God had called them.

In his 90th book *Metahuman: Unleashing Your Infinite Potential*,[25] Deepak Chopra advises humans to go beyond human constructs and connect with their innate beings. He points out that our collective kind has brought climate decline, extinction of species, poison in our food chain, nuclear weapons, interference with democracies through internet hacking. It looks like we are planning our extinction. We have the technologies to reverse these trends but do we have the collective will? This requires a spiritual shift. A simple contemplative practice can lead us into this shift.

The heart of the monastic way is the imitation of Christ in all things. People are deeply attracted to true humility. To see Jesus in the poor. The only time Jesus refers to people as his family is in the context of love of the poor.

Breakdowns are an opportunity for breakthrough. These latter day Brendans are already among us. They have his humility to discern the Creator's imprints in what is here. They grow in his qualities until fresh Bethlehems, villages of God and places of resurrection grow in our own

---

24. The Community of Aidan and Hilda Way of Life.

25. Chopra, *Metahuman*

soil. These new Brendans also teach Euro-Americans how they may make restitution to native peoples.

Tom and Nancy Gilbert, who purchased plots of land near a river at a place they call Hermits Cove in Oregon, are an example of how acts of reconciliation can be practical. Before he paid for his new house he dreamed that he should ask the original Indian owners for permission. Congress does not recognize any Indian tribe in that area, but Tom researched and tracked down two local descendants of the Nehalem tribe that was nearly wiped out by disease. (In 1898 the Nehalem, or Tillamook, became the first tribe to sue the US government for compensation for the lands they had taken.) They held council with other survivors and gave permission. Tom donated them the amount in dollars that he had paid for his property.

A medieval Irish monastic Rule which the anonymous author attributed to Saint Columba requires "forgiveness from the heart towards all". During the presidency of George W. Bush, a group of chiefs went to the Whitehouse and offered forgiveness to non-Native Americans. A representative group of non-Native Americans now needs to offer an apology for the mistreatment of Natives. The national apology by Australian's former Prime Minister, Kevin Rudd, for the White Australians' mistreatment of its Aboriginal tribes set a healing process in motion. One of my friends and an Aboriginal mate were there, both in tears. They embraced.

Someone in ministry to indigenous people wrote this letter to me: "I don't know whether I could bear to hear one more story of pain: It is just too painful what "white men" have done to them. I can't sleep at night and I am awakened in the middle of the night thinking how a broomstick was used to harm our friend when he was only five years old and to all the other children at the boarding school. And he still suffers with his health sixty years as doctors cannot help what's been damaged inside of his body. And this boarding school was sponsored by the church. He said it happened to every single child at that boarding school. It is easy to say, "Forgive and move on," but it is another thing to be tormented sixty years later. I almost told him that he was lying because I just could not believe. Our brother FORGAVE even when these perpetrators never asked for forgiveness; he said that he did not want to live in bitterness and anger. What a beautiful thing it is when we could forgive! We need to let our Native American friends talk because they need to be heard. If God puts you in Native American ministry (or any ministry), this is something you must do, I believe the ability to forgive someone is by bringing history into the light from darkness of their souls. And this often take many years!"

People like Will and Millie Toms have already given years of their life in the service of this call. It is hard, as Millie has shared in her writings.[26] Yet Millie and Will are not only faithful servants: even when depressing things happen to those among whom they have labored, and when everything seems to break down, they are inspired connectors across the world. Millie believes that so much Christianity is canned, and that we must not put God in a box. She writes "I truly believe we are a ragamuffin bunch of people, who are daring to step out to dream and do what we feel the Creator of the universe is calling us to do!" So, they also go to the Melanesian Islands, to Hawaii, the Caribbean, and to First Nation peoples in Australia.

Will and Millie Toms believe that the non-Christian world will respond to Jesus through the witness of First Nation peoples more than through western Christians who have forfeited credibility, and through Euro and African Americans who learn from them the arts of deep listening.

This belief was reinforced when they led a delegation of Hopis to meet with Aboriginal tribes near Sidney, Australia. They bonded and sparked like never before. The late Billy Graham said, "The greatest moments of Native history may lie ahead of us if a great spiritual awakening should take place. The Native American has been a sleeping giant. He is awakening. The original Americans could become the evangelists who will help win America for Christ!"[27]

The meeting point between the white Acquisitive Society and the native Acquiescent Society is not in a high place, where people sell their souls to climb the ladder of success; nor in churches which promote mission as merely a set of beliefs or a productivity drive in the name of Christ. It lies in the opening of the eyes to The Way which, although it has been overlaid, is already here among us.

Chief Luther Standing Bear refers to this as "a fundamental and spiritual law": "The attempted transformation of the Indian by the white man and the chaos that has resulted are but the fruits of the white man's disobedience of a fundamental and spiritual law. "Civilisation" has been thrust upon me since the days of our reservations, and it has not added one whit to my sense of justice, to my reverence for the rights of life, to my love for truth, honesty and generosity or to my faith in Wakan Tanka, God of the Lakotas."

26. Ehn-Toms, *Great Eagle Rising*.
27. Twiss, *One Church Many Tribes*, 24.

Warren Petoskey an Elder and spiritual leader among the Odawa and Lakota Nations says. "We Indian people have survived five centuries of near-constant assassination and extermination attempts. We have survived genocide, chemical and germ warfare, terrorism, sterilisation, relocation, reservations, urbanization, boarding schools, orphanages and the foster care system, all of which were designed to erase the consciousness of what it means to be an Indian in North America . . . I believe we are here today not because of the benevolence of a controlling government, but because the Creator has willed it so."

Could it be that the Creator has willed it so because he wants Indian, White, and African Americans to give up their idolatrous pursuits and ego-projected expressions of religion, and return to being Followers of the Way—like the first disciples of Jesus?

Voyage Together to a Shared Future

Many native people feel it is too late. They are locked into a conflicted existence that is neither one thing nor another. They can never go back to their way of life before the white settlers came, yet neither are they happy to deny their roots and be swallowed up in hollow white society. Some, such as those who work with the Indigenous Messengers International, network widely, but such a calling is not for everyone. Many white people either shrink into a fortress Christianity, writing off everyone who is outside it, or they reject Christianity as an outdated expression of empire. The Return of Brendan offers a third way. It invites all people to voyage with integrity, remaining true to the sacred essence of their inheritance while recognizing that a season has passed, being open to the Great Spirit in those who travel alongside them, whether they are White or Black, Native or Hispanic.

Such a fellow-traveling has been prophesied. In 1880 Bear Clan Chief Loololma from the village of Oraibi held up two strings and prophesied: "This string is the Hopi way of life. The other is the good things of the white man's way of life". He tied the two strings together. "Combine both and the Hopi people will be twice as strong".

Richard Twiss writes: "A growing number of evangelical Native believers are using the term "the Jesus Way" to describe their faith in Jesus Christ. This phrase speaks of a way of life, a trail we walk on and live by. South Lakota people speak of Jesus as *Chanku*, "the Road" or "the Way". Jesus said of Himself, *"I am the way, the truth, and the life"* (John 14:6). The Jesus Way presents Jesus Christ to the unbelieving Native in terms that are more in line with the way Native people approach life. Among nonbelieving Indians the word "Christianity" has come to mean only the abusive religion of the White man".[28]

The psychologist C J Jung identified that part of us, as individuals and as peoples, that he called The Shadow. This is the part of us that we repress and don't wish to acknowledge. Jesus likened it to *"whitewashed tombs which on the outside appear beautiful, but inside are full of dead people's bones and all uncleanness."* Matthew 23:27. The treatment of the Indian tribes by White America cries out to heaven. It reveals the blindness, arrogance and false models at the heart of so-called Christian America. It is also a way to enter into The Shadow with humility and courage and to find transformation.[29]

The circle speaks into this situation, too. Indians who were brought into white churches did not understand church buildings with rows of hard wooden benches and people staring at the backs of others heads, with one person doing all the talking and being paid for it. There are diverse theories about the circle in the Celtic Cross, but one thing is clear: a circle is not straight rows. A circle speaks of community. The early Celtic churches were communities. This, too, is an important element in the "Brendan factor"— as we pause in our journey together we gather in circles, not straight rows.

New voyagers spread the word about Celtic Spirituality and won't rest until Aidan and Hilda, the spiritual mothers and holy people among tribal elders are as well known in USA as Saint Patrick. The desert fathers and mothers, and people inspired by them in Britain in later centuries, agreed with people who are against oppression but they also were honest about themselves. They admitted that there is a dictator inside themselves waiting for an opportunity to get his/her own way. So, we new voyagers try to get rid of bitterness, blame, bossiness, and despair.

New voyagers sail away from fragmentation towards greater wholeness. They are weavers. They know that they cannot undo "colonial Christianity" from the top, but they can let something new grow from the grass-roots. The Community of Aidan and Hilda, has stated: "As we study the history of the Celtic Church (that is early churches in Celtic lands) we rediscover the unity we had as one Christian people within the one universal church. We are constantly ashamed of our divisions, and we repent of the schisms

28. Twiss, *One Church* 24

29. Simpson, *Prayer Rhythms*, 44

that have occurred between the eastern and western church and from the Reformation onwards . . . we seek to weave together the God-given strands in Christianity which have become separated." The cloth of dualistic Christianity has been torn into shreds. God is weaving a new cloth.

The new voyagers refuse to abdicate responsibility for business and economics. Why should the devil have all the best enterprise? In the Bible the word economy (oikonomia) refers to a dispensation of good stewardship. An oikos means a household, and nemo to its management. The whole global system is described as God's oikos in Ephesians chapter 1. We are called to manage it as stewards, as in Jesus's parables of the vineyard labourers (Matthew 20) and the unjust steward (Luke 16). So, economics in God's eyes is about managing the world household for the benefit of everyone in it and for the glory of God. Theologians such as Ched Myers have called for a new narrative of American capitalism. At a 2009 conference he said it has transformed economic exchange from something that was supposed to serve social and ecological relationships to something that now demands their sacrifice. In the introduction of his book The Biblical Vision of Sabbath Economics[30] Myers states that God's people are instructed to dismantle, on a regular basis, the fundamental patterns and structures of stratified wealth and power, so that there is "enough" for everyone. This is relational economics.

Australia and Canada both publicly apologized in 2008 for their mistreatment of their indigenous peoples. In the US a sort of apology was signed into law in 2009 but was buried in the Defense Appropriations Bill.[31] A full-hearted, prime-time apology supported by the churches would do much to bring "the Brendan factor" to the fore-front.

If we wanted to express this movement of new Brendans in biblical terms we might see ourselves as members of The Order of Melchizedek. Melchizedek, an indigenous priest in Bible lands, welcomed Abraham, Melchizedek stood in the land as a type of God's general revelation to all. As priests of the land, Native Americans can welcome and bless those who come in obedience to God and bring a revelation whose fullness is found in Jesus –the Jesus of every people and in all creation.

With Walt Whitman we voyagers declare:

> "Allons! we must not stop here. However sweet these laid-up stores, however convenient this dwelling we cannot remain here,

30. Myers, *Biblical Vision*
31. Capriccioso, "*A sorry saga*".

However shelter'd this port and however calm these waters we must not anchor here, However welcome the hospitality that surrounds us we are permitted to receive it but a little while.

Allons! the inducements shall be greater, We will sail pathless and wild seas, We will go where winds blow, waves dash, and the Yankee clipper speeds by under full sail . . .

Allons! after the great Companions, and to belong to them! They too are on the road—they are the swift and majestic men—they are the greatest women, Enjoyers of calms of seas and storms of seas, Sailors of many a ship, walkers of many a mile of land, Habitués of many distant countries, habitués of far-distant dwellings, Trusters of men and women, observers of cities, solitary toilers, Pausers and contemplators of tufts, blossoms, shells of the shore, Dancers at wedding-dances, kissers of brides, tender helpers of children, bearers of children, Soldiers of revolts, standers by gaping graves, lowerers-down of coffins, Journeyers over consecutive seasons, over the years, the curious years each emerging from that which preceded it, Forth-steppers from the latent unrealized baby-days, Journeyers gayly with their own youth, journeyers with their bearded and well-grain'd manhood, Journeyers with their womanhood, ample, unsurpass'd, content, Journeyers with their own sublime old age of manhood or womanhood, Old age, calm, expanded, broad with the haughty breadth of the universe, Old age, flowing free with the delicious near-by freedom of death. all that was or is apparent upon this globe or any globe, falls into niches and corners before the procession of souls along the grand roads of the universe. Forever alive, forever forward . . ."

With Rarihokwats of the Mohawk Nation we declare:

"Indigenous spirituality is not a religion. It is a way of being. It is a way of understanding the natural world that gives us life. It is a way that guides our conduct. It is understood differently by each living creature. Some human beings may not understand it at all. Developing that understanding is a task that is before us all and continues from birth, and maybe before death, and maybe after. It cannot be taught. But it can be learned. Each of us has our own obligation, if we wish to accept it. If we wish to be open to finding it. This quest is what makes life a journey, not a destination."

Rarihokwats, was a citizen of the Mohawk Nation at Akwesasne, and a member of the Bear Clan. He is the founder of Akwesasne Notes—at that time the largest native newspaper in the world. He was a visiting professor at the University of Ottawa.

New voyagers set aside weights that hold them down and run their course spurred on by the heavenly cloud of witnesses (Hebrews 12:1). New voyagers look not to the things that are behind but *"press on to take hold of that for which Christ Jesus took hold of us"* (Philippians 3:12).

New voyagers know this:

> If there be righteousness in the heart, there will be beauty in the character
> If there be beauty in the character there will be harmony in the home
> If there be harmony in the home there will be order in the nation.

When there is order in each nation there will be peace in the world.

New voyagers look for opportunities to bless what they see around them. Brendan sought and gave blessings. Saint Patrick famously pronounced a blessing over Munster: "A blessing on the people of Munster; a blessing on the land that gives them food; a blessing on the chiefs, on the homesteads, slopes and levels . . ." It is said that people who follow the Celtic ways bless "every blessed thing". In that spirit, I invited people on a retreat on England's Holy Island of Lindisfarne to write prayers of blessing for 24/7 things in this age of machines and internet. These were printed in my book *Celtic Blessings: Prayers for Everyday Life*.[32] Above all we bless the land.

Daniel Christian Wahl, a consultant on bio-regional regeneration, writes: "Our future depends not just on a re-inhabitation of our bioregions but also on a re-indigenisation of our way of being . . . Our bioregional Indigenous ancestors always knew that we belong to the land rather than the land belonging to us"[33]

An Aboriginal Activist Group in Queensland displays this poster: "If you have come to help me you are wasting your time. But if you have come because your liberation is bound up with mine, then let us work together."

This is the meaning of Brendan's return voyage. This is Christ's desire. This is the Way. This is the new American Dream.

---

32. Simpson, *Celtic Blessings.*
33. Resurgence & Ecologist Issue 321

A Selection of Books by Ray Simpson

Aidan of Lindisfarne: Irish Flame Warms a New World (Wipf and Stock)

Celtic Blessings: Prayers for Everyday Life (Loyola)

Celtic Christianity and Climate Crisis (Sacristry)

Celtic Christianity: Deep roots for a modern Faith (Anamchara New York)

Daily Light from the Celtic Saints—Ancient Wisdom for Modern Life
(Anamchara New York)

Hilda of Whitby—a spirituality for now (Bible Reading Fellowship)

A Pilgrim Way: New Celtic Monasticism for Everyday People
(Kevin Mayhew)

Prepare the Way: Celtic Prayers for the Season of Light
(Anamchara New York)

St. Aidan's Way of Mission—Celtic Insights for a post-Christian world
(Bible Reading Fellowship)

Tree of Life: Celtic Prayers to the Universal Christ (Anamchara New York)

For a full list of resources and on-line purchases see his web site
http://www.raysimpson.org/store/type/book

Bibliography

Bell, Rob. *Heresy, holiness, and Oprah: Rob Bell interviewed* https://soundcloud.com/user-632063010/rob-bell-on-life-after-love-wins-preaching-and-comedy-trump-and-more

Berry, Thomas. *The Sacred Universe: earth, spirituality and religion in the twenty-first century*, Columbia University Press 2009.

Bonhoeffer, Dietrich. *"Letter to Karl-Friedrich Bonhoeffer (January 14, 1935),"* in *A Testament of Freedom: The Essential Writings of Dietrich Bonhoeffer*, Geffrey B. Kelly, and F. Burton Nelson, eds. revised edition New York: HarperCollins, 1995.

Boyd, Gregory. A *Lies My Teacher Told Me* www.gregboyd.org/blog/lies-my-teacher-told-me

Brueggemann, Walter. *The Prophetic Imagination* Fortress 40th Anniversary Edition 2018.

Budden, Chris. *Why Indigenous Sovereignty Should Matter to Christians*, Mediacom Education Inc., 2018.

Cameron, Ian. *Lodestone and Evening Star: the seamen who mapped the world*, Hodder and Stoughton 1965.

Capriccioso, Rob. *A sorry saga: Obama signs Native American apology resolution*, Indian Country Today https://indiancountrytoday.com/archive/a-sorry-saga-obama-signs-native-american-apology-Ko_2JdB5vkea3lUmULTZEg

Charleston, Steven. *The Four Vision Quests of Jesus* Morehouse 2015.

Chopra, Dr Deepak. *Metahuman: Unleashing your infinite potential.* Rider 2019

Church, Casey. *His Holy Smoke: The Contextual Use of Native American Ritual and Ceremony*, Cherohala 2017.

Coles, Robert. *The Spiritual Life of Children* Houghton Mifflin Boston 1990.

The Community of Aidan and Hilda. *The Aidan Way* Issue 98 August 2020

————. *Way of Life.*

Converging Pathways. *Call to Action #60.* https://convergingpathways.ca/action/?ID=211

Davies, Oliver ed. *Celtic Spirituality* The Classics of Western Spirituality Series New York Paulist 1999

Dawson, John. *Healing America's Wounds* International Reconciliation Coalition, Native American Chapter of North America, P.O. Box 1417, Castle Rock, CO 80104.

Drane, John W. *The McDonaldization of the Church: Spirituality, Creativity and the Future of The Church*, Darton, Longman & Todd UK ed. 2000.

Eastman, Charles Alexander (Ohiyesa). *From the Deep Woods to Civilisation*, University of Nebraska Press 1977.

Ehn-Toms, Millie Camille. *Great Eagle Rising: True Confessions of a Missionary* iUniverse 2011.

Flower, Robin. *The Irish Tradition*, Oxford University Press 1978.

Friesen, Jeff, and Steve Heinrichs, eds. *Quest for Respect: The Church and Indigenous Spirituality (Part of Intotemak Trilogy)* Commonword 2017 https://www.commonword.ca/ResourceView/82/19134

Geeze Magazine Fall 2015 issue.

Ghazarian, Jacob G. *The Mediterranean Legacy in Early Celtic Christianity: a journey from Armenia to Ireland*, Bennet & Bloom 2006

Hancock, W. Neilson, Thaddeus O'Mahony et al, eds. *Senchus Mor Ancient Laws of Ireland* (6 vols) Dublin 1869 https://www.vanhamel.nl/codecs/Hancock,_et_al._1865–1901

Holland, Tom. *Dominion: The Making of the Western Mind* Little, Brown 2019.

Joyce, Timothy. *Celtic Christianity: A Spiritual Tradition for Today,* Orbis 1998.

King Jr, Martin Luther. *Where Do We Go From Here: Chaos or Community?* Harper & Row 1967.

Kingsolver, Barbara. *Sheltered* Harper Perennial 2019.

Kopenawa, Davi and Bruce Albert. *The Falling Sky: Words of a Yanomami Shaman* Harvard University Press 2013

Kruger, C. Baxter. *The Great Dance: the Christian Vision Re-visited* Perichorersis 2011

———. *Jesus and the Undoing of Adam*, Perichorersis 2011.

Lowe, Jeanine Leblanc. Indigenous Hospitality: Gaining Wisdom and Learning Practices from Cultures that Welcome Journal of North American Institute for Indigenous Theological Studies Volume 7 2009.

Lyons Lee, Brent and Ray Simpson. *Celtic Spirituality in an Australian Landscape*, St. Aidan Press

Mayhew-Smith, Nick. *The Naked Hermit: a journey to the heart of Celtic Britain* SPCK 2019.

McIntosh, Alastair. *Hell and High Water: Climate Change, Hope and the Human Condition*, Birlinn 2012.

Meyer, Kuno. *Selections from Ancient Irish Poetry* Trieste Publishing 2017.

Mance, Henry. *The Rise and fall of the office* Financial Times 15th May 2020

Men, Father Alexander. *The Wellsprings of Religion: the history of religion—in search of the Way, the Truth and the Life*, St. Vladimir's Seminary Press 2017.

Mercier, Hugo and Dan Sperber. *The Enigma of Reason: a new theory of understanding*, Allen Lane 2017

Murray, Jim. *A Wasicu (White Man) in Indian Country* Xlibris 2012

Neihardt, John G. *Black Elk Speaks.* New York: Pocket 1972.

Nerburn, Kent. *Voices in the Stones: Life Lessons from the Native Way* New World Library 2016.

———. *The Wisdom of the Native Americans*, New World Library 2010.

Newell, J. Philip. *Christ of the Celts* Jossey Bass Wiley 2008.

Paul, Daniel N. *We were not the Savages: First Nations History* Fernwood 2007.

Peterson, Eugene. *Christ Plays in Ten Thousand Places, Eat This Book, Practise Resurrection* Waterbrook 2015.

Pope Francis. *Gaudete et Exultate* (Rejoice and be Glad) Veritas 2018.

Pope John Paul II. *Address to Native Peoples of the Americas* (September 14, 1987). Full text at http://w2.vatican.va/content/john-paul-ii/en/speeches/1987/september/documents/hf_jp-ii_spe_19870914_amerindi-phoenix.html

Project Implicit. *Harvard Implicit Bias Test https://implicit.harvard.edu/implicit/*

Bibliography

Raven, Sea. *'The Wheel of the year-A worship book for Creation spirituality'* PhD Diss The University of Creation Spirituality Oakland, California 2001 Quoting Neihardt, John G *Black Elk Speaks,*

Reed, Simon. *Followers of the Way: ancient discipleship for modern Christians,* Bible Reading Fellowship 2017.

Resurgence & Ecologist Issue 321 July/August 2020

Sanneh, Lamin. *Disciples of All Nations Oxford Studies in World Christianity,* Oxford University Press 2008

Scazzero, Peter. *The Emotionally Healthy Leader: How Transforming Your Inner Life Will Deeply Transform Your Church, Team, and the World,* Zondervan 2015.

Schaeffer, Francis A. and Udo W. Middelmann, *Pollution and the Death of Man* Crossway 1992

Schlesinger Jr, Arthur W. *The Vital Center: The Politics of Freedom* Routledge 1997

Schmidt, Wilhelm and Fritz Bornemann. *Der Ursprung der Gottesidee* (The origin of the idea of God), Aschendorff 1926.

Schmidt, Wilhelm. *The Origin and Growth of Religion* Translated by H J Rose, Wythe-North Publishing 2014

————. *High Gods in North America (Upton Lectures in Religion, Manchester College, Oxford),* Clarendon 1933

Scott, James C. *Dominion and the Arts of Resistance: Hidden Transcripts,* Yale University Press 1992.

Severin, Tim. *The Brendan Voyage* Gill and Macmillan 2005.

Sharpe, Richard ed. *Adomnan, Life of St. Columba* iii. 17 Penguin Classics 1955.

Simpson, Ray. *Celtic Blessings: Prayers for everyday Life,* Loyola 2003.

————. *Celtic Christianity: Deep Roots for a Modern Faith* Anamchara Books 2016.

————. *The Cowshed Revolution: A new society created by downwardly mobile people,* Kevin Mayhew 2011.

————. *High Street Monasteries: Fresh Expressions of Committed Christianity* Kevin Mayhew 2019.

————. *Hilda of Whitby: a spirituality for now,* Bible Reading Fellowship 2014

————. *Liturgies from Lindisfarne* Kevin Mayhew 2020.

————. *New Celtic Monasticism for Everyday People with Study Guide,* Kevin Mayhew 2014

————. *Prayer Rhythms for Busy People* Kevin Mayhew 2005.

Simpson, Ray and Brent Lyons Lee. *St. Aidan's Way of Mission: celtic insights for a post-Christian world* Bible Reading Fellowship 2016.

Smith, Adam. *The Theory of Moral Sentiments,* Penguin Classics 2010.

————. *The Wealth of Nations* Simon & Brown 2012.

Smith, Huston. *The World's Religions: Our Great Wisdom Traditions,* Harper Collins 1986.

Sparks, Paul, Tim Soerens and Dwight J. Friesen. *The New Parish: How Neighborhood Churches Are Transforming Mission, Discipleship and Community,* Inter-Varsity Press 2014

Stengel, Richard. *Information Wars: How We Lost the Global Battle Against Disinformation & What We can Do About It* Atlantic Monthly 2019.

Stubbs, William, Arthur West Haddan and David Wilkins. *Councils and Ecclesiastical Documents Relating to Great Britain and Ireland* Volume 2, part 2 Oxford University Press 1873.

Bibliography

Sugirtharajah, R S. *The Bible and the Third World: Precolonial, Colonial, and Postcolonial Encounters*. Cambridge University Press 2008.

Twiss, Richard. *One Church Many Tribes: Following Jesus the Way God Made You*, Regal 2000.

———. *Rescuing the Gospel from the Cowboys: a native American expression of the Jesus Way*, Inter-Varsity Press 2015)

Vile, John R ed. *The Constitutional Convention of 1787: A Comprehensive Encyclopedia of America's Founding* ABC-CLIO, 2005.

"Who Was John Muir?" Sierra Club, http://www.sierraclub.org; John Muir, The Yosemite New York: Century, 1912.

White Jr., Lynn. *The Historical Roots of our Ecological Crisis* Science, New Series, Vol. 155, No. 3767 1967 http://www.cmu.ca/faculty/gmatties/lynnwhiterootsofcrisis.pdf

Willard, Dallas. *The Divine Conspiracy* HarperCollins 1998.

Woodley, Randy. *Living in Color: embracing God's vision for ethnic diversity*, Inter-Varsity Press 2010.

———. *Shalom and the Community of Creation: An Indigenous Vision* Wm. B. Eerdmans 2012.

Wright N T. *The Day the Revolution Began*, HarperOne 2016.

Zahnd, Brian. *Water to Wine: some of my story* Spello 2016.

Lightning Source UK Ltd.
Milton Keynes UK
UKHW021023231221
396125UK00005B/73